Legal Ethics

Occupational Ethics Series

Elizabeth Beardsley and John Atwell,
Series Editors

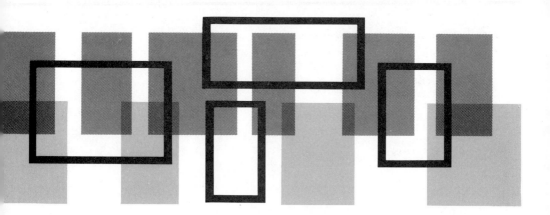

Legal Ethics

KENNETH KIPNIS

University of Hawaii at Manoa

PRENTICE-HALL, Englewood Cliffs, New Jersey 07632

Library of Congress Cataloging-in-Publication Data

Kipnis, Kenneth.
   Legal ethics.

   (Occupational ethics series)
   Bibliography: p. 109
   Includes index.
   1. Legal ethics—United States.   I. Title.
II. Series.
KF306.K57 1986   174'.3'0973   85-25727
ISBN 0-13-528118-0

© 1986 by Kenneth Kipnis

Printed in the United States of America

10 9 8 7 6 5 4 3 2 1

ISBN 0-13-528118-1   01

PRENTICE-HALL INTERNATIONAL (UK) LIMITED, *London*
PRENTICE-HALL OF AUSTRALIA PTY. LIMITED, *Sydney*
PRENTICE-HALL CANADA, INC., *Toronto*
PRENTICE-HALL HISPANOAMERICANA, S.A., *Mexico*
PRENTICE-HALL OF INDIA PRIVATE LIMITED, *New Delhi*
PRENTICE-HALL OF JAPAN, INC., *Tokyo*
PRENTICE-HALL OF SOUTHEAST ASIA PTE. LTD., *Singapore*
EDITORA PRENTICE-HALL DO BRASIL, LTDA., *Rio de Janeiro*
WHITEHALL BOOKS LIMITED, *Wellington, New Zealand*

For Samuel and Lola Kipnis

Contents

Prentice-Hall Series in Occupational Ethics

An increasing number of philosophers are coming to appreciate the value of making our discipline constructively available to those whose lives are chiefly focused on some form of practical activity. It is natural that philosophers specializing in ethics should be in the forefront of this movement toward "applied philosophy." In both writing and teaching many leading ethical theorists are currently dealing with concrete issues in individual and social life.

While this change has been taking place within the philosophic community, practitioners in various fields have (for several complex reasons) turned their attention to the ethical dimensions of their own activities. Whether they work in areas traditionally called "professions" or in other occupations, they wish to consider their job-related decisions in relation to ethical principles and social goals. They rightly recognize that many, if not most, ethical problems facing all of us arise in our occupational lives: We are often expected to conduct ourselves "at work" in ways which appear to conflict with the ethical principles believed valid in other social relationships; in our occupations themselves certain normally accepted practices sometimes seem to contradict each other; in short, ethical dilemmas of enormous proportion face the morally conscientious person. Whether philosophical ethics can help resolve these acute problems is an inescapable question.

A third recent development is the growing tendency of students to think of themselves as persons who do or will have certain occupational roles. This tendency is noticeable at several stages of life—in choosing an occupation, in preparing for one already chosen, and in pursuing one that has been entered some time ago.

The convergence of these three contemporary developments has created a need for appropriate teaching materials. The *Occupational Ethics* Series is designed to meet this need. Each volume has been written by a philosopher, with the advice or collaboration of a practitioner in a particular occupation. The volumes are suitable for liberal arts courses in ethics and for programs of preprofessional study, as well as for the general reader who seeks a better understanding of a world that most human beings inhabit, the world of work.

John E. Atwell and Elizabeth L. Beardsley, Editors

Preface

Most writings on legal ethics have a cautionary tone. As a largely self-regulating profession, the organized bar has, over the years, promulgated a series of codes of ethics and has participated as well in their enforcement. There were the Canons of Professional Ethics, which were replaced by the Code of Professional Responsibility, which was in turn superseded by the Model Rules of Professional Conduct. Because members of the legal profession can be disciplined for the violation of these rules—even barred permanently from the practice of law—attorneys may unknowingly place themselves at risk if they are unfamiliar with the prevailing code's requirements. Simple prudence—what lawyers call "covering your ass"—may require that practicing attorneys have a working knowledge of professional ethics, especially those sections of the code where violations can have serious professional repercussions. This is especially true where attorneys use the strictures of the code as offensive weapons, hobbling their adversaries and threatening them with disciplinary action to gain advantages for their clients in litigation.

Much of the rest of the writing on legal ethics has about it the tone of the muckraker. The central concern of these authors is to unmask and demystify a profession in which, allegedly, self-righteousness and elitism conceal corruption and sociopathology. Various charges are characteristically made: that lawyers too often share in the guilt of the culpable people they defend; that they routinely wrong others in serving their clients; and that, at the expense of justice for the less well off, they promote the interests of those who can afford the legal services of powerful firms. Sometimes the critics treat the codes as essentially irrelevant to the bar's culpability: With respect to the most pressing ethical problems, the codes are silent. Sometimes the codes themselves are the target, explicitly licensing or even requiring practices that can damage the lawyer's moral personality and contravene the public interest.

Yet another species of writing on legal ethics is celebratory in tone. In countless Law Day speeches and law school commencement addresses, the bar and its pantheon of heroes are trotted out and hailed as champions of the unpopular and the downtrodden. The legal profession stands at its post, guarding and preserving the most fundamental values in Western civilization: justice, liberty, fairness, due process, reason, the dignity of the individual, and the rule of law.

The book you hold in your hands does not fit comfortably into any of these categories. Though I have learned much from the cautionary writings and from the bar's continuing efforts to hammer out its codes of professional ethics, this work is not intended to help aspiring attorneys avoid disciplinary action. I have tried to avoid the lawyer's tendency to turn moral dilemmas into questions of statutory and legal interpretation, the inclination to seek one's professional standards exclusively in the black letters of the codes and in the reasonings of the formal opinions. Those who seek the bright line separating that which the profession permits from that which it prohibits will be better served if they look elsewhere.

Nor is it my intention to rip the lid off the chicanery of the profession and to show once and for all how it conspires against the laity. The pages that follow hold no brief for the prosecution of the profession and its membership. More broadly, this is not an empirical study of lawyers. Though there is much to be gained by the examination of the extensive literature describing and excoriating the bar, my intention has not been to add to it.

Nor is it the purpose of this book to raise yet another cheer on behalf of our learned brethren at the bar. To be sure, what lawyers do is important. And there is something to be learned from those who have endeavored to clarify the distinctive social values that are realized in the work of skilled and honorable attorneys. But although the bar's social contribution merits its fair measure of recognition and appreciation, lawyers' work seems to me no more vital than, for example, what parents, plumbers, teachers, and philosophers do. Nor do lawyers as a class have a corner on virtue and dedication. Heroism and integrity can be found and appreciated in many walks of life; they are not more precious for distinguishing lives in the law.

Instead, the chapters that follow speak of and to a profession that is ethically troubled, a profession that does not possess a clear, shared sense of how to engage the many moral dilemmas that arise in legal practice. In the present era, the roots of the debate are entwined with the events that have come to be called "Watergate," events in which many lawyers, including the president of the United States, were involved. In the years since Watergate, the legal profession has begun to place unprecedented emphasis on professional responsibility, both in legal education and in its examinations for admission to the bar. There has been a thorough review of the profession's code of ethics; and a controversial new set of principles, the Model Rules, has been put forward. The chapters that follow were written within this spirit of reflection. The aim is to provide an overview—what Wittgenstein called a "perspicuous representation"—for key ethical problems that arise for practicing attorneys. A secondary purpose has been to make progress, philosophically, toward the resolution of some central problems of professional responsibility in law and, more broadly, to illustrate how the intellectual strategies of philosophy can fruitfully be brought to bear upon these issues.

Some readers may be surprised that so little of what follows pertains to criminal practice, the area of law that seems most to have captured the public imagination.

Only about a third deals with that topic; the rest concerns corporate practice, wills, divorce, tort liability, and so on. But though it is more prominent in the public eye, criminal law is only a small part of what law students study in law school and an even smaller part of what legal practice is generally about. Accordingly, the emphasis here is on civil practice, but with due attention to the problems of confidentiality and complicity that are somewhat unique to criminal law.

As one who is not an attorney, who therefore has never practiced law, and who has no professional self as a lawyer to defend or impugn, I have drawn upon a diversity of somewhat unusual sources in preparing this work. Though not a matriculated law student, I had the opportunity of spending a year at the Law School of the University of Chicago, more or less loitering in the presence of legal education. I was able, while at Chicago, to learn to access legal literature and to understand something of the tedium, panic, exhilaration, and crushing disappointment that are part of legal education and practice. I have shared an important part of my life with Sara Lyn Smith, now an attorney working in Honolulu. Because of that association, I have had a rich picture of the experience of legal education and practice. My participation in 1977 in the Council for Philosophical Studies Summer Institute on Law and Ethics, funded by the National Endowment for the Humanities, put me in contact with many of those lawyers and philosophers whose names appear in this book. That experience was invaluable as this work proceeded. I have been a member of several academic grievance committees and have had more than a glimpse of the importance of due process. As chair of an institutional review board for the protection of human research subjects, I have come to appreciate the importance of codified procedure. As an elected member of the board of directors of a union of academic professionals, I have dealt with attorneys engaged in representing our 2,400-member organization and have seen the value of the work that lawyers do at the appellate level. And having been involved in contested legal proceedings myself, I have had firsthand experience with the virtues and vices of our system of adjudication. In much of this I have endeavored to get a sense of the lawyer's distinctive role in our society, while at the same time, as a philosopher, keeping a professional distance from identification with the subject matter.

It would be difficult to mention all those who have contributed to the present work. A full list would include teachers, friends, relatives, colleagues, judges, law professors, attorneys, and a slew of authors whose opinions were at hand as this book was written. But among the very many whose comments about earlier versions of the work are reflected in what I have judged to be improvements in this version, a few stand out as meriting special recognition. Among these are David Luban, Elizabeth Dvorkin, Andrew Kaufman, Bruce Landesman, Fred Elliston, Lisa Newton, Andrew Jameton, Sissela Bok, Robert F. Ladenson, Haskell Fain, Michael Martin, Albert Flores, Lawrence Heintz, Baird Kidwell, and Michael Bayles. I am indebted to Sonia Fabrigas and Kathleen Hallisey for their valuable assistance in the research connected with this work, and to Wendy Ford for her help in preparing the manuscript for publication.

Chapter 1

The Concept
of Professional Responsibility*

In an influential article published in 1975, Richard Wasserstrom called attention to what he took to be a troublesome conflict between the ethical standards of the legal profession and the more familiar standards that are applicable to nonprofessionals.

> Conventional wisdom has it that where the attorney-client relationship exists, the point of view of the attorney is properly different—and appreciably so— from that which would be appropriate in the absence of the attorney-client relationship. For where the attorney-client relationship exists, it is often appropriate and many times even obligatory for the attorney to do things that, all other things being equal, an ordinary person need not, and should not, do.[1]

For Wasserstrom, and for many others who have worried about legal ethics, the question is "whether this particular and pervasive feature of professionalism is itself justifiable."[2] It is, I believe, important to observe that Wasserstrom's question is posed by the very existence of professional codes of ethics. For if the codes are not mere reiterations of "ordinary morality"—and, indeed, they are not—one wants to know how a different set of ethical standards can be applicable to a discrete group of people. Ethically speaking, what makes "I am a lawyer" an excuse or a justification for actions that would otherwise be morally questionable, or worse? What makes lawyers so special?

At least two important traditions in moral philosophy strongly suggest that the quest for an answer to this question is fundamentally misconceived. In Immanuel Kant, for example, the distinguishing characteristic of sound ethical principles is

---

*Earlier versions of this chapter appeared in *The University of Dayton Review*, 15, no. 2 (Winter, 1981–1982): 69–78; and in Wade L. Robison, Michael S. Pritchard, and Joseph Ellin, eds., *Profits and Professions* (Clifton, N.J.: Humana Press, 1978). Copyright by Kenneth Kipnis. Reprinted by permission of the publishers. In addition, some passages are adapted from Kenneth Kipnis and Gailynn Williamson, "Nontreatment Decisions for Severely Compromised Newborns," *Ethics* 95 (October 1984): 90–111.

[1] Excerpted from Richard A. Wasserstrom, "Lawyers as Professionals: Some Moral Issues," *Human Rights*, 5, no. 1 (1975): 1–24. Copyright 1975 by the American Bar Association. Reprinted by permission of the American Bar Association, Section of Individual Rights and Responsibilities, and the author.

[2] Ibid., p. 6.

their universal applicability.[3] To have moral worth, an action must conform to principles that could govern the conduct of all rational agents. Kant's basic idea is that in reasoning about our conduct, we should consider that any answer to the moral question "What ought I to do?" must equally be an answer to the question "What ought all rational beings to do?" Taken literally, the Kantian approach rules out the possibility of a sound "local" moral code. There can be no correct ethical standards that are applicable to any fewer than all persons. Since the legal profession's distinctive code of conduct is, supposedly, a special moral code for lawyers, either Kant is mistaken in believing sound ethical principles to be universalizable, or attorneys are wrong in believing their special code to consist of sound ethical principles.

Among the utilitarians there is an equally troublesome tradition for those who defend any lawyer's code of ethics. Moral philosophers such as John Stuart Mill[4] have argued that sound ethical reasoning must consider equally the interests of all who might be affected by alternative courses of conduct: That course of action is favored which maximizes the general happiness. But lawyers working in the adversary system are characteristically bound by the strictures of their role to serve as partisan advocates for their clients. In reasoning about their obligations as attorneys, advocates—by definition—must weight the interests of their clients more heavily than the interests of other parties. Attorneys are simply not supposed to be even-handed in taking into account the interests of all. While impartiality may be the proper intellectual stance for a judge, it is not an appropriate professional posture for an advocate. Thus either utilitarians are mistaken in believing that sound moral reasoning must be impartial in its consideration of affected interests, or attorneys are mistaken in believing that partisan advocacy is morally permissible.

But, as Wasserstrom noted in his 1975 article and as other commentators have since observed, lawyers and other code-regulated professionals are not alone in claiming to be subject to special ethical standards.

> Being a parent is, in probably every human culture, to be involved in role-differentiated behavior. In our own culture, and once again in most, if not all, human cultures, as a parent one is entitled, if not obligated, to prefer the interests of one's own children over those of children generally. . . . If one were trying to decide what the right way was to distribute assets among a group of children all of whom were strangers to oneself, the relevant moral considerations would be very different from those that would be thought to obtain once one's own children were in the picture. In the role of parent, the claims of other children vis-à-vis one's own are, if not rendered morally irrelevant, certainly rendered less morally significant. In short, the role-differentiated character of the situation alters the relevant moral point of view enormously.[5]

---

[3] Immanuel Kant, *Fundamental Principles of the Metaphysic of Morals* (Indianapolis: Bobbs-Merrill Educational Publishing, 1949).

[4] John Stuart Mill, *Utilitarianism* (Indianapolis: Hackett Publishing Company, Inc., 1979).

[5] Wasserstrom, "Lawyers as Professionals," p. 4.

In a sense, to become a parent is to alter one's moral universe. It is to assume a role to which, *contra* Kant, special ethical standards apply; a role within which, *contra* the utilitarians, a moral privilege obtains to attend more carefully to the interests and needs of some persons (your own children) than might otherwise be justified. For parents, and for those occupying other roles as well, morality in action is, as Wasserstrom puts it, "role-differentiated." As he explains the term, behavior is role-differentiated when it is appropriate for the agent to set aside considerations—even moral ones—that would otherwise be relevant or decisive. The role of the agent has to be taken into account in assessing conduct. In becoming a parent, for example, one comes to have special responsibilities, and these special responsibilities may properly enter into our moral evaluation of the behavior of persons occupying the role. These special responsibilities are characteristically connected with correlative privileges.

This notion of "privilege" calls for an explanation. Three points need to be made. First, privileges are special rights and liberties that are carved out of the rights and liberties of others. Just as the driver of an ambulance exercises a privilege when, in activating lights and siren, he violates the speed limit and obliges other motorists to pull over to the side, so parents may restrict what would otherwise be the liberty of children—their children's rights to act as they choose. Privileges are an extension of the rights of some into what would otherwise be the rights of others. Second, society grants these privileges for public purposes. We are all more secure because ambulance drivers have their special privileges. Likewise, the purpose behind the public acknowledgment of parental privilege would appear to be to secure for children the important benefit of maturing into healthy, responsible adults. Social recognition of parental authority reflects a common judgment that the public interest in the protection and nurturance of children is thus served. Finally, these privileges are revocable for reasons of abuse, neglect, or inability to meet the correlative responsibilities. If the ambulance driver takes advantage of his privileges in order to be on time for a movie, if he ignores urgent calls for help, or if he becomes disabled and cannot do his job, he is relieved of his responsibilities and, with them, his correlative privileges. So it is with parents who abuse or neglect their children or who for other reasons are unable to care for them. Important matters of concern should not be entrusted to persons who are clearly not in a position to attend to them.

It is special responsibilities and privileges such as these that make the moral difference, that skew the ethical standards properly applicable to attorneys away from those that have traditionally commanded the attention of philosophers like Kant and Mill. For attorneys, as for many other professionals, the moral problems of professional practice call for a sound appreciation of the diverse responsibilities attaching to their role, both the sources of those responsibilities and their scope. Because concepts like having a responsibility, being a responsible person, and being responsible (as for some mishap) are so central in the study of legal ethics, it will be helpful to take up these topics at the very outset.

CONCEPTS OF RESPONSIBILITY

Let us begin with the idea of having a responsibility.[6] A married couple has responsibility for the welfare of their child. A philosophy instructor has responsibility for a particular course. A particular member of a mountaineering expedition has responsibility for the maps. The sanitation company has responsibility for the proper collection and disposal of a community's garbage. Lawyers typically have responsibility for the affairs of their clients. In these cases and others, what one has responsibility *for* is always a matter of some concern. One would have to know the whole story in order to explain how it is that someone has responsibility for, say, a pebble; why, for example, it is a pebble of considerable importance, a crucial piece of evidence in a criminal case. In general, the more important the matter of concern, the greater the responsibility.

Those who have responsibility for matters of concern are expected (in the evaluative, not the predictive, sense of "expected") to give these matters all the attention due them. They are expected to be able to provide—and can generally be called on to provide—an account of how they are ensuring that due care and attention are being given to the matters of concern for which they have responsibility. When we talk about an agent's responsibility, we are referring to a sphere of concern for which that agent is accountable. If a preventable mishap occurs within the sphere, there is a strong presumption that the agent is blameworthy. This concept of a responsibility—a sphere of concern for which an agent is accountable—is the concept I am taking to be fundamental here. To distinguish it from two derivative concepts of responsibility to be sketched shortly, I will refer to it as "substantive responsibility."

Not every agent is well suited to assume substantive responsibilities. A derivative concept of responsibility—what I will call "virtue responsibility"—is applied to persons who, in a particular way, are well suited to assume important substantive responsibilities. Of the responsible person, Graham Haydon has written:

> He will . . . be aware that he stands in, or has the opportunity of entering into, certain relationships with certain others in such a way that he in particular can be called to give an account of what happens in certain specified spheres. But in recognizing that he can be called to account for the nature and outcome of his actions, he is recognizing . . . the importance of so acting as to be able to give a good account.[7]

Thus the responsible person will be one who takes seriously the act of assuming a substantive responsibility and who, having assumed it, can be counted on to give that responsibility the care and attention it is due.

Conversely, the person who is irresponsible is one who is predisposed to careless-

---

[6] The discussion here builds on H. L. A. Hart's analysis of "role responsibility" developed in Chapter 9 of his *Punishment and Responsibility* (New York: Oxford University Press, 1968).

[7] Graham Haydon, "On Being Responsible," *Philosophical Quarterly* 28 (1978): 56.

ness and/or inattention to responsibilities. It is not difficult to understand why irresponsibility is generally regarded as a vice. Many of our activities are undertaken within the contexts of relationships and organizations requiring a high degree of mutual reliance. The settling of responsibilities within the relationship or organization is often necessary if the actions of the participants are to make sense. Consider two pilots flying a large aircraft over the sea. If each attends to the need for coordination, progress can be made in safety. But either can, through inattention, frustrate the good-faith efforts of the other, endanger third parties, and in general erode the trust that makes cooperation possible in the first place. When we determine that a person is irresponsible, we typically relieve that person of responsibilities and refrain from delegating new ones.

A second derivative sense of responsibility should be noted. If the child suffers because of the neglect of its parents, if the philosophy course serves only to convince students of the pointlessness of the discipline, if the maps for the mountaineering expedition are damaged or misplaced, if the lawyer misses a filing date, we may hold certain persons responsible for these mishaps: It is their fault. What I like to call "mishap responsibility" can occur in two ways: An individual may act so as to bring about the mishap, or an individual with substantive responsibility for a matter of concern may, by neglecting to give due care or attention, allow the mishap to occur. When mishaps occur, people with substantive responsibility for relevant matters of concern are routinely called on to provide accounts of themselves.

It appears to be a fact of contemporary life that concerns about irresponsibility will generally be related to whether or not a mishap has occurred and, in addition, to the scale of the mishap. The first major nuclear accidents provoked a penetrating interest. However, where the irresponsibility is clear and the risk of serious loss is high, then, even if no mishap results, concern may well be great. If a flight crew throws a drunken party while aloft in a loaded aircraft, interested persons in authority may well take a hard look at the personnel and the procedures of the airline in question.

A word needs to be said about the way in which one comes to have responsibilities. In the clearest cases, responsibilities are more or less explicitly settled by the parties themselves or by their authorized representatives. There are matters of concern that must receive attention, and there is a group of persons who create or maintain a system of relationships—an organization or organized activity—such that the responsibilities and the means of meeting them are allocated in a reasonable manner. Settling responsibilities is an ongoing process. Questions often arise about the privileges, rights, resources, immunities, and status accorded to those with responsibilities. These concomitant benefits and privileges can be significant incentives for individuals to assume important responsibilities, and they are subject to forfeiture when these same individuals are relieved of their responsibilities. Accordingly, disagreement about how to attend to matters of common concern may mask conflict about whose special interests will receive the most abundant satisfaction. Beyond the issue of benefits, there are questions about the standards to be met in attending to responsibilities; questions about the quality of past performance; and finally, questions about how responsibilities ought to be delegated—whether, for example, those who have them ought to be relieved of them.

Consider, for example, the responsibility of parents for their children. It is profoundly important that children be cared for, and the institution of the family is the prevailing means by which this care is expressed. The legal and social context of parenthood accords privileges, rights, resources, immunities, and status to persons who are parents so that the welfare of children is ensured. As things now stand it is up to parents, first of all, to see to it that their children mature into adults in a wholesome way. A failure here may thus be a moral failure, a failure to meet one's responsibilities in a context in which significant social values are at stake. In cases of such failure, where parents are shown to be unfit for the task of child rearing, they are relieved of their responsibilities by the courts.

Consider the member of the mountaineering expedition with responsibility for the maps. Just as others in the group rely on that individual to attend to this important matter, the map carrier can rely on companions to attend to other remaining concerns. If, however, it turns out that the map carrier cannot be relied on, prudence requires that he or she be relieved of responsibilities in this context. Here, as with parenthood, responsibilities are more or less explicitly delegated. There is a reliance upon the person with responsibility, a granting of benefits in recognition of that responsibility, and the option of relieving the agent of responsibility when the arrangement proves unsatisfactory.

It should not be difficult to understand the lawyer as working within a framework of such substantive responsibilities. To be sure, attorneys have important responsibilities to clients. In addition they may have responsibilities to co-workers: peers, superiors, and subordinates within a firm or agency, for example. They also have major responsibilities to the judicial system within which they do their characteristic professional work. And, finally, they have a collective responsibility for upholding the quality of the legal profession. It is to this concept of collective responsibility that we now turn.

COLLECTIVE RESPONSIBLITY

If one thinks of substantive responsibility in this general way, collectivities as well as persons may have responsibilities. For example, the sanitation company can, through authorized representatives, enter into an agreement with an incorporated township. If the agreement provides that the sanitation company have the exclusive right to pick up and dispose of the garbage, and that the township make available consideration in return for these services, then it seems unproblematic that the company has the responsibility for picking up the garbage in the township.

But now suppose that the garbage does not get picked up—let us say the company discovers that it does not have the resources to meet its responsibilities under the terms of the agreement. Can we not make sense out of the suggestion that the company itself—as opposed to particular persons working within it—might be "irresponsible"?[8] To be sure, there clearly are cases in which the failure of an organization to meet its responsibilities is a consequence of the failure of a particular person within the organization to meet his or her responsibilities. But the matter cannot rest here, for an organization is more than a collection of persons: It is a system of positions and associated procedures. Thus, if an irresponsible person occupies a position and, as a consequence, a mishap occurs, it may be that the *procedures* used to select persons to occupy positions of responsibility *are themselves defective* in some way. It is also possible, even when each person within the organization meets his or her responsibilities, that *because the structure of the organization itself is faulty, its responsibility is not met.*[9] Perhaps the structure impedes the flow of certain types of information. Perhaps certain matters are not assigned as anyone's responsibilities. Perhaps the organization trains its personnel to attend only to some aspects of a problem, neglecting others; or only takes on persons who follow that pattern; or singles them out for promotion, eventually discarding the others. One response might be that in these cases the irresponsibility should be charged against whoever originally designed the structure of the organization. But organizations rarely have such architects; they are often mere agglomerations of positions and procedures that have accumulated gradually over the years. (Such structures may lack a coherent justification. We can only explain them as the products of historical processes.) And even where a defect-ridden organization can point to its architect, one might still wonder how the responsibility for design happened to settle on a person so deficient in organizational competence!

Although we may not be comfortable talking about organizations as "irresponsible," there can be no doubt that some of them are predisposed to carelessness and inattention toward the responsibilities they have assumed. Social institutions are artifacts, instruments that people have fashioned to realize human values. As with any other artifact, they may be fashioned with care and skill, or they may be object lessons in negligence, irresponsibility, and even viciousness. If one is concerned with the propensity of a particular organization to fail to meet its responsibilities, one cannot afford to overlook the structural aspects of the problem. In a society that routinely delegates to organizations responsibility for a broad range of matters of public concern, close attention should be given to the manner in which persons within those organizations are selected, trained, promoted to positions of authority, and constrained to organize themselves so as to give due attention and care to our concerns. In the following section I will show how it is the delegation of such responsibility that creates a profession.

---

[8] The issues surrounding organizational irresponsibility are helpfully represented in Christopher D. Stone's *Where the Law Ends* (New York: Harper & Row, Publishers, Inc., 1975).

[9] The general issue of collective, nondistributive responsibility is treated in Peter A. French, ed., *Individual and Collective Responsibility* (Cambridge, Mass.: Schenkman Publishing Co., Inc., 1972). See especially the articles by R. S. Downie and David Cooper.

COLLECTIVE RESPONSIBILITY
AND PROFESSIONALISM

The development of an occupation into a profession is a lengthy process.[10] Occupations may be located at virtually any point along a continuum, with day laborers at one end and doctors and lawyers at the other. Nevertheless, three distinct but related features characteristically emerge as professionalism progresses.

1. In the first place, organized practitioners within an occupation begin to make a *claim to maximal competence.* Through their representatives, one begins to hear that persons belonging to a certain discrete class, because of their intense and thorough intellectual training and practical experience, exceed in skill all other persons in a particular area of endeavor. Two conditions must be satisfied before such a claim can be made. First, there must be some organization of practitioners within the favored class. The organization need not include all of them, but must include enough to warrant a claim to speak on behalf of the whole class. Second, there must be some criterion for deciding who belongs to the class of favored practitioners and who does not. In the end, this evolves into an elaborate gatekeeping procedure involving education, accreditation of schools, and certification of new members. The esoteric nature of the knowledge and skill possessed by this select class of practitioners begins to make it look as if persons outside the favored class simply lack the capacity to make sound judgments about the performance of those specialists. As the claim to maximal competence comes to be accepted, it begins to seem more and more reasonable to let the select class of practitioners certify and evaluate itself. The organization of favored practitioners stands ready to assume this responsibility.

2. The special competence possessed by members of a profession is of a sort that can be applied to some matter of public concern. For reasons that will become clear, the process of professionalization requires that the profession make a public *commitment to devote itself to the realization of some significant social value.*[11] The members of the profession must undertake to give due attention to the distinctive matter of social concern to which its skills and knowledge can be directed. Typically one finds explicit reference to these values in the preambles to the codes of ethics that emerge from professional organizations. Thus, the American Bar Association's *Code of Professional Responsibility* begins with the following:

> The continued existence of a free and democratic society depends upon recognition of the concept that justice is based upon the rule of law grounded in respect for the dignity of the individual and his capacity through reason for enlightened self-government. Law so grounded makes justice possible, for

---

[10] See Harold Wilensky, "The Professionalization of Everyone," *The American Journal of Sociology* 70 (1964): 137.

[11] See Talcott Parsons, "Professions," *International Encyclopedia of the Social Sciences* 12 (1968): 536. It is often noted that professions have a "public service orientation."

only through such law does the dignity of the individual attain respect and protection. Without it, individual rights become subject to unrestrained power, respect for law is destroyed, and rational self-government is impossible.

Lawyers, as guardians of the law, play a vital role in the preservation of society. The fulfillment of this role requires an understanding by lawyers of their relationship with and functions in our legal system. A consequent obligation of lawyers is to maintain the highest standards of ethical conduct.

The same type of self-identification can be seen in official statements from professions of less lofty pretension. Consider these words from the preamble to the Code of Ethics of the National Association of Real Estate Boards:

> Under all is the land. Upon its wise utilization and widely allocated ownership depend the survival and growth of free institutions and of our civilization. The Realtor is the instrumentality through which the land resource of the nation reaches its highest use and through which land ownership attains its widest distribution. He is the creator of homes, a builder of cities, a developer of industries and productive farms.
>
> Such functions impose obligations beyond those of ordinary commerce. They impose grave social responsibilities to which the Realtor should dedicate himself, and for which he should be diligent in preparing himself. The Realtor, therefore, is zealous to maintain and improve the standards of his calling and shares with his fellow-Realtors a common responsibility for its integrity and honor.[12]

These examples can be multiplied.[13] Only rarely, however, do professional associations precisely delimit the social values to which their skills are characteristically to be directed and to which they pledge to commit their energies. Nonetheless, what is clear is that professions characteristically endeavor to represent themselves as dedicated to an ideal of social service.[14]

3. Neither the competence nor the commitment is sufficient to change a discrete organized occupational activity into a profession. What is needed is *social recognition of and reliance on the organized profession* as the means by which certain skills are to be applied and certain matters of public concern given the attention they are due. This last feature is built on the preceding two. For if there is confidence that the members of a profession possess maximal competence in a particular area, and if there is trust that these practitioners are deeply committed to the responsible application of their distinctive skills, there will seem to be neither the ability nor the

---

[12] Quoted in Stephen J. Martin, ed., *Commentaries on the Code of Ethics* (Bloomington: Indiana University Press, 1974), p. v. I am grateful to Mary Carson Smith for calling this material to my attention.

[13] An excellent collection of professional codes, many with preambles like those cited, is to be found in Jane Clapp's *Professional Ethics and Insignia* (Metuchen: Scarecrow Press, Inc., 1974).

[14] In the end this produces a distinctive type of transaction in the payment of fees to professionals. They are paid, not for their work, but rather in order that they may do their work. Lawrence Haworth develops this point in his *Decadence and Objectivity* (Toronto: University of Toronto Press, 1978), p. 112.

need to designate nonprofessionals as overseers of professional practice. No one is competent to do the job; moreover, it does not need to be done in the first place.

As this view becomes more plausible, as the profession earns or otherwise secures public trust and confidence, it gradually obtains autonomy at both the institutional and the individual level. Institutional autonomy is secured when the organization obtains recognition as representing the profession. It is invited to speak on behalf of the profession. It takes control over membership: the selection and training of candidates, the accreditation of professional schools and programs, the certification of new members, the promulgation and enforcement of standards of professional practice. In the clearest cases of professionalization—law and medicine—the profession becomes, in essence, an unregulated legal monopoly with respect to a certain service, unauthorized practice being a criminal offense. Individual autonomy is secured when the profession obtains a substantial measure of control over the conditions and content of its work. It lays claim to, and is granted, the latitude it asserts that it needs in order to do its best job. Autonomy for the individuals in a profession can take several forms. The tradition of academic freedom is probably the best-known mechanism, but others can be seen, for example, in the governance structures of hospitals,[15] and in the operation of Disciplinary Rule 3 of the ABA Code of Professional Conduct, which effectively prevents lawyers from working for nonlawyers in corporations that sell legal services. In each context, substantial control over the conditions and content of work is secured by members of the affected profession.

In the end, of course, it is we who, through our representatives, delegate responsibility to professions or relieve them of it. With respect to professions as a whole and the communities they serve, responsibilities are settled, in some cases, in committees of state legislatures. These committees typically meet with the representatives of professional organizations in an effort to hammer out satisfactory arrangements. In the case of the legal profession, professionalization is largely the creature of the judiciary. Although the "right to counsel" was secured in the Constitution, the modern lawyer appeared when judges began to allow a certain privileged group to come "before the bar" (a physical bar, separating the public from those with business in the court) for the purpose of representing (as opposed to counseling) paying clients. The granting of this privilege to those who had been "admitted to the bar" and the subsequent criminalization of the "unauthorized practice of law" secured for the legal profession a privilege as important as any that has been granted to a profession.

It has not been established that the delegation of such responsibility is necessarily unwise.[16] Much, it seems, depends on the political dimensions of the institutional and individual autonomy that is granted, the soundness of the profession's claim to competence (the scope of that competence relative to the legitimacy of the

---

[15] I am grateful to Andrew Jameton for calling the matter of hospital governance to my attention.

[16] Milton Friedman presents a strong case in "Occupational Licensure," in *Capitalism and Freedom* (Chicago: University of Chicago Press, 1963).

knowledge-claims on which it is based), and the degree to which the profession is genuinely committed to an ideal of public service. A complete justification of a profession would necessarily take account of all of these matters. Here, however, what is of most interest is the commitment, for it assures us that the privileges that have been granted will not be exercised irresponsibly. If the profession plainly has organized itself in such a way as to ensure that its distinctive matter of social concern receive from the profession the attention it is due, then it may well be reasonable for us to choose to maintain a system of professional practice.

PROFESSIONAL ETHICS

We come then to the ethics of the profession. Codes of ethics embody a theory about the relationship between the profession and the community it serves: Lawyers, it will be remembered, are "guardians of the law." The codes indicate in their preambles the significant social values that the professions take to be their primary concerns. Although there is often a pressing need for the precision that philosophical skills could provide, the central intent is clear: to register, on the part of the profession, an official recognition of the sphere of responsibility to which the profession owes due attention.

But how, we may want to know, is this recognition of responsibility—the reciprocal of social privilege—to be acted upon by the organized profession? One way is by instituting a code of ethics, a set of principles defining the conditions under which professional skills are to be applied. Naturally, at some point we would want to consider the mechanisms by which a profession ensures that its members conform to its principles. These mechanisms might include enforcement procedures, educational programs in professional ethics, and tests for good moral character. In any case we would want to be assured that they were adequate to provide substantial adherence to the code of ethics under the existing conditions of professional practice. For a justifiable professional code consists of principles that, if substantially adhered to, would guarantee that the substantive responsibility of the profession receive the attention it is due. The rationality of the delegation of responsibility to professions can thus turn on the soundness of those principles.

Consider, for example, the duties that arise when someone makes it clear that he or she is committing a serious wrongdoing that is punishable by law. Assume that this takes place in a situation in which the one who is apprised of it is expected not to divulge the information. Should the proper authorities be notified? In a nonprofessional context one can envision the arguments going either way. But if it is a doctor who receives the information while acting in a professional capacity, then the following argument would have application.

Doctor-patient confidentiality is one of the best-known and most firmly established principles in medical ethics. It is embodied in the Hippocratic oath, and its special claims on the medical profession are recognized in legal privilege.[17] The

---

[17] See, for example, Rule 27 of the Uniform Rules of Evidence.

justification for this principle is reasonably clear. In our society the medical profession has a special responsibility for the health of the community it serves. Persons who are not medical professionals usually lack the skill and confidence that doctors have; and even if nonphysicians were competent, they are barred by law from putting their knowledge and skill into practice. The granting of special privileges to the medical profession would lack point in the absence of a reasonable expectation that the members of the profession were undertaking to use those privileges to serve (rather than to exploit) the public. Doctors have indeed been quite successful in their efforts to encourage the public to rely exclusively on their profession in attending to certain concerns. For the medical profession to meet its responsibility, the public must be willing to see doctors when the need arises and to supply information that doctors need if the latter are to do their best work. It is reasonable to suppose that if doctors—even a very small number of doctors—feel free to use that information to the detriment of the patients who supply it, the public will be less than willing to cooperate with doctors. A betrayal of confidence by a medical professional can quickly erode public trust and poison the environment in which medical practice flourishes. On the other hand, adherence to the principle of doctor-patient confidentiality helps to create the environment in which the medical profession can do its best job.

Construed in this general way, the special responsibilities of individual professionals are based on the responsibilities their professions have assumed in the process of professionalization. And, if this account is apposite, the principles of professional ethics—some of them, at least—can be justified as sets of rules substantial adherence to which will create an environment in which due care and attention are best given to the distinctive matters of concern for which professions are maintained.

It is important to note here that small changes in the articulated commitment of the profession can produce great changes in the code of ethics. Thus some disputes about what appear to be ethical issues may mirror deep differences concerning what the commitment of the profession ought to be. Consider, for example, the obligations that arise when a doctor believes that the small child being treated has been battered by the parent who brought her in. Assume that, although it is possible for the doctor to save this child from further harm by notifying the proper authorities, if the doctor does this, other child abusers will hesitate before taking their injured children to doctors, with consequent fatal results for some of these other children. Still other parents will hesitate to seek treatment out of fear that, if they bring their injured children to the doctor, they will be wrongly identified as child abusers. Now, on one account, the doctor ought to be the champion of the abused patient. The medical profession should assert its overriding obligation to the patients who are delivered to its hands. Nothing can be more important than the suffering patient who is being attended by the doctor, and the interest that patient has in securing physical well-being. The physician should report the case to the authorities out of a concern for this patient. Yet on a second account, the medical profession is the means by which we express our concern for our physical well-being. The medical profession that does the best job is the one that best secures the health of the community it serves. Thus, although at the outset some children may be better helped by the doctor's notifying the authorities, in the long run a medical profession that routinely betrays parents will lose the trust it must have if it is to do its best work. Nothing can be more important to a doctor than to be worthy of trust. On the first account the medical profession is primarily concerned with the health of its patients. But on the second account the concern is with the general physical well-being of the community. A resolution of the ambiguities in the present codes may press hard choices upon the professions, their membership, and those who delegate responsibilities to them.

Although other matters need to be considered, it is clear that the codes merit close attention in the philosophical study of professional ethics. They delineate the public interest which the profession exists to serve. Sound codes set out principles that, if substantially adhered to, will ensure that the public interest will receive from the profession due care and attention. The claim that sound principles have upon the practitioner has its basis in the claim that the profession has to the trust of the public. A responsible profession, one might say, is one that does not merely profess its dedication to the public interest in its code but in addition expresses that dedication in its very constitution.

From the point of view of the individual professional, this way of looking at things highlights the political role that practitioners must play within the profession itself. As a member of a profession, as one who can participate in its governance, he or she shares responsibility for the quality of its structure. If that structure merely serves to create the illusion of concerned attention, if it serves values that are quite different from—or even at odds with—the values the profession claims to serve, then the need is great for effective political action within the profession.[18]

From the point of view of the citizen, this way of looking at things highlights the power of the public to delegate responsibility to professions and to relieve them of responsibility. Deprofessionalization, the process of relieving professions of their responsibilities (and the concomitant privileges and benefits), has been urged by some critics.[19] At a minimum, prudence requires that one refrain from leaving important matters to organizations that are predisposed to inattention as regards the responsibilities they have assumed. The code of ethics of a profession is a guarantee that the practice of individual professionals will conform to principles that display due regard for the profession's sphere of responsibility. Given the extent of our reliance upon the professions, it would not be unreasonable to subject these guarantees to the most rigorous philosophical scrutiny.

[18] Obstacles in the way of effective political action may be substantial within the profession itself. The structure of many professions precludes significant participation by large and distinct segments of its membership: the AAUP and nontenured professors, the American Bar Association and sole practitioners, the various engineering professional associations and working (non-managerial) engineers.

[19] See, for example, the writings of Ivan Illich: *Deschooling Society* (New York: Harper & Row, Publishers, Inc., 1972); *Tools for Conviviality* (New York: Harper & Row, Publishers, Inc., 1973); and *Medical Nemesis* (New York: Pantheon Books, 1976).

But the guarantees of the codes must be understood in terms of the professional's role in society. It is not as if Kant and Mill were wrong. Rather, as an independent field of study, professional ethics begins at the point where these traditional approaches leave off. What they leave out is the philosophical elucidation of the socio-political context within which much of our moral reasoning takes place. The hardest questions in professional ethics involve the characterization of the social context of professional practice: The traditional approaches do not typically consider the ways in which roles—being a parent, for example—play a proper part in moral reasoning. Thus, before one can begin to assess a profession's code, one must have a sense of the professional's social position. In the case of the legal profession, it is necessary to understand at the outset the lawyer's function in the judicial system and, even more fundamentally, the function of the judicial system in society. This last question must be dealt with first. If the choice of an adversary system is warranted, that may be a strong justifying reason for a unique, systematically necessary set of ethical standards for lawyers. But even if the adversary system is not justified, it does not follow that lawyers are free to ignore the responsibilities and obligations they now have. For, using parents again as an example, suppose it were conclusively shown that other means were better suited to the task of rearing children than the institution of parenthood. Suppose we knew that grandparents did the job much better. Even if it were demonstrated that parents were not deserving of the special rights and responsibilities they presently have, parents would still have those rights and responsibilities, both legal and moral, because they are, I would say, built into the present social structure; they should be respected, at least until that structure is changed. If the adversary system is not a reasonable method of adjudication, it does follow that it may be obligatory for lawyers working within the system to move toward replacing it with a better one. It does not necessarily follow, however, that lawyers may wholly ignore their obligations within that system while it is still in effect.

The philosophical study of professional ethics must therefore begin with political philosophy: In order to understand legal ethics, we must begin with the justification of the adversary system, within which lawyers do their characteristic work.

Chapter 2

Lawyers in the Context
of the Adversary System

The distinctive work that lawyers do, they do in the context of a set of procedures that have been developed for the resolution of certain types of disagreement. To understand the ethical dimension of the lawyer's practice, it is necessary to understand both the informing purposes and the basic structure of our judicial system and to appreciate the place within it of the legal profession. But to describe in any detail a modern court system would be a task for a book many times the size of this one. And to justify that system—in terms of defensible, choiceworthy social values—would be an even larger task. And so what follows can be only the barest outline of a fuller account. But, sketchy as it is, the picture here should suffice. Our judicial system is an artifact that we have crafted with important common purposes in mind. It has an architecture that can be roughed out in a few lines that need not be false to their subject matter. And while a more complete justification cannot be attempted here, one can indicate why the choice for this or that basic feature has been deemed reasonable (as well as why it might be thought unreasonable). In the end, it is the purpose of this chapter to establish the *plausibility* of the judgment that our present system of adjudication—an adversarial system involving judicial independence, the doctrine of precedent, and judicial accountability—is a sound one and, further, to have laid the groundwork for the detailed discussion of professional ethics to be taken up afterwards.

TWO TYPES OF DISAGREEMENT

We begin with a story. Potter and Watson are neighbors; not, however, friendly neighbors. In the interest of their privacy, both would like to have a barrier of some sort on the boundary separating their two adjacent lots. Although they are willing to share the costs of constructing and maintaining the barrier, they have not been able to settle on the kind of barrier to be erected. Because she is fond of the flowers that would grow upon it, Potter wants a dense hedge. But because Watson desires more security than a hedge would provide, he wants a tall wooden fence. Both Potter and Watson are clear about the advantages of cooperation: Each would enjoy reduced costs and also additional space. (The barrier could be erected on the border

15

rather than entirely on the land of either one.) But alas, they have not been able to agree on a mode of cooperation.

At last, Watson decides to act on his own. He begins to erect, wholly on his own property, a twenty-foot-tall wooden fence and prepares to paint it orange. Potter, seeing what Watson is up to, lets him know of her objections. The tall fence will cast a fatal shadow on many of her beloved flowers and plants. It will completely spoil her view of the trees and hills that would still have been visible over a shorter structure. Her solar water heater, which she recently installed at considerable expense, will now be useless. And the color of the fence not only is one she dislikes intensely; it makes the fence an eyesore that will depress the market value of her house and other houses in the neighborhood.

Watson listens to Potter's objections but disagrees with what she says. Since he is building the fence with his money on his property, he believes he can do as he pleases. Indeed, he points out, Potter did not solicit his permission when, several months earlier, she went ahead and planted daffodils in her backyard. He has had to look at her daffodils ever since they came up. (Watson doesn't actually mind the appearance of daffodils, but he doesn't see that that makes any difference.) In the same way, he feels that he does not need Potter's permission to put up his fence, even though she will have to look at it. Potter pleads that it is wrong for Watson to spoil her enjoyment of her property; that Watson does not have the right to build a fence that is so objectionable, so intrusive upon her reasonable concerns as the owner of the adjacent property. He replies that the land on which the fence stands is his, and that, regardless of Potter's preferences, he has the right to build the fence upon it. Out of an initial failure to agree has emerged a dispute. The issue now is whether or not Watson has the right to build the fence he is constructing.

It is helpful at this point to distinguish the two successive disagreements between Potter and Watson. In the first—the disagreement over the nature of the common barrier—the differences between the parties have made it impossible for them to arrive at a common plan. Potter's preferred plan is not the same as Watson's, and neither is willing and/or able to give up special advantages in order to secure the common benefits of cooperation. Note that neither party is claiming that the other has an obligation to go along with his or her idea. Put another way, neither claims a right to the other's compliance. Both are seeking a formula for cooperation, but there are limits to what each is willing to contribute to the effort.

Contrast the above disagreement with the second. In the dispute over Watson's fence, there is disagreement over the rights the parties enjoy as property owners. Watson claims that as a property owner he has the right to construct and paint his fence as he chooses, given that it is wholly on his land. Potter, on the other hand, claims that Watson's right to build on his property is limited by her rights not to have the plants on her land die from want of light, not to have her view obstructed, not to have her sunlight permanently blocked, not to have her solar collector cast into the shade, not to have her quiet enjoyment of her land spoiled, and, lastly, not to have the market value of her property lowered by an eyesore. Both Watson and Potter identify themselves as landowners; they base their conflicting judgments on their differing views of what is involved in landownership. For Watson, owning land means that in general he is not obliged to take into account the interests of anyone else when he decides what he wants to do with it. For him, the erection of the fence is a wholly innocent exercise of his rights of ownership. But for Potter, owning land means that others have to take into account certain of her interests when they decide to act; that she has rights that others cannot violate. For her, the construction of the fence constitutes a kind of trespass. Unlike the first disagreement, the second involves a question about the rights of the parties.[1] For convenience, let us stipulate a distinction between "failures to agree," where the question involves whether and how cooperation will take place; and "disputes," where the question centers on the rights of the parties.

How might the initial failure to agree—over the nature of the desired common barrier—be settled? The first thing to note is that it need not be settled at all. A failure here can mean no more than that there won't be cooperation: Neither Watson nor Potter will enjoy the benefits that agreement would bring. Now clearly some level of cooperation is necessary in any community. There will inevitably be problems whenever people live in close proximity to one another, problems which affect the community as a whole and which can best be dealt with by means of some kind of concerted effort. There will be persons who commit serious wrongdoings and who pose a threat to the community. Problems will arise in connection with sanitation and with the maintenance of paths and other common elements. There will be opportunities as well to improve the general quality of life. Perhaps the community can convene in some kind of general meeting, or perhaps it can constitute a legislature and somehow authorize it to deal with certain common problems and to pursue certain common goals. But however necessary cooperation may be at the community level, not much of consequence will be lost if Potter and Watson are unable to find a common path. Not every germinating seed of cooperation need flourish. But even though Potter and Watson are not here required to cooperate, how might agreement be secured anyway?

Potter and Watson might reach agreement through *reasoned discussion.* They might jointly inquire about the best way to meet their varied preferences. Perhaps there is a type of fence that would permit Potter to enjoy the flowers she would like to see at the edges of her yard. Perhaps there is a flowering shrub that will provide Watson with the security he desires. Maybe it can be shown that neither a fence nor a hedge is such a good idea after all. Reasoned discussion depends on a shared desire to arrive at the best answer. It is itself an important—perhaps the most important—form of cooperation. Of course there may not be sufficient time or

[1] This is not to say that the rights question is the only one present in the second dispute. Each of the parties might well be concerned about the neighborliness of the other: whether Watson is being spiteful or Potter intolerant and unreasonably contentious. A more discerning eye might well focus solely on the fact that the two seem to have so little regard for each other. Why, we might choose to wonder, are they both so interested in building barriers in the first place? To restrict ourselves to the rights question may well be to blind ourselves to issues of greater importance. As any lawyer knows, there are many ways to frame the issue in a conflict.

knowledge or skill to reach agreement, or perhaps the parties simply have too many irreconcilable needs or ideas about how cooperation should take place. Reasoned discussion carries with it no guarantee that a mutually satisfactory agreement will emerge, at least not in the short run in which human beings live their lives.

The parties might well engage in *negotiation*. They might pursue the kind of bargaining one associates with exchanges. If Watson agrees to share in the cost of planting the flowering shrubs that his neightbor desires, Potter will assume all the costs of maintenance. Alternatively, if Potter agrees to a fence, Watson will build it wholly on his land: Potter will have more usable yard space for her plants. Negotiations can involve threats as well as bribes: Potter might threaten to plant ragweed, aggravating Watson's allergy, unless Watson agrees to a hedge. In practice, negotiation and reasoned discussion are often difficult to distinguish. One may not be sure whether the other party has difficult-to-satisfy sensibilities or is strengthening a bargaining position by taking a hard opening line. It is easy for those experienced in negotiation to lose faith in the possibility of reasoned discussion.[2]

But, having failed to reach agreement by talking with each other directly, Watson and Potter might agree to *mediation*. They might bring in a third party, someone they both respect, who can help them to formulate a mutually acceptable plan. While Watson and Potter may have come to doubt each other's good faith, they are more likely to trust the good faith of a well-respected mediator, one who is working for both parties in an effort to bring them together. By talking privately with Potter and privately with Watson, the mediator can explain, reason, cajole, chastise, persuade, and often, in the end, help the two to appreciate each other's concerns and thus come to agreement. Mediators possess important skills that are not utilized as often as they might be.

Another approach is *arbitration*. As with mediation, arbitration requires the two to agree to bring in a third person. But with arbitration, Potter and Watson further agree to let the arbitrator decide the issue between them; they will abide by the decision of the arbitrator, whatever it turns out to be. (There might be some limits to the authority granted to the arbitrator; for example, he or she might be required to choose between the last offers of the parties to the disagreement.) To be effective, the arbitrator should be someone both Potter and Watson respect, someone who cannot be suspected of favoring one side over the other. One widely used arbitration procedure would provide a list of five arbitrators. Potter and Watson would take turns crossing names off the list until only one remained. After listening to both sides, the chosen arbitrator would issue a decision that each had agreed to treat as binding.

There are many variations on negotiation and arbitration. Negotiation can be handled by negotiating agents rather than being carried on directly through the parties. There can be an arbitration committee with representatives from both sides as

---

[2] Legislatures are very much in the business of hammering out arrangements for cooperation. And it is no surprise that reasoned discussion and negotiation are the standard means by which such efforts are made.

well as an impartial arbitrator. If people have a strong enough interest in cooperating, in formulating a common plan, there are many ways to facilitate their success.

But matters differ substantially in the second disagreement, the dispute turning on Watson's claimed right to build the tall orange fence on his land. We have a situation here in which one party, Potter, believes that rights—rights that are important to her—are being violated. It is not merely a case of one party failing to cooperate with another. It is that Watson, in attempting to realize a benefit for himself, has overstepped what Potter takes to be the bounds of tolerability. Recollect that in the earlier failure to agree, all of the mechanisms for securing agreement—reasoned discussion, negotiation, mediation and arbitration—depended on both parties having an interest in identifying a mutually acceptable mode of cooperation. But here, while Watson may continue to desire the goodwill of his neighbor, he may feel that there are strict limits to Potter's right to tell him how he must arrange things in his backyard; limits that are, in his opinion, clearly exceeded by her objections to his fence. While she may be sincere, he cannot take her intrusiveness seriously. His interest in cooperation with Potter being at an end, he decides to ignore her complaint. Thus reasoned discussion, negotiation, mediation, and arbitration cannot apply here, for each presupposes a bilateral interest in cooperation, an element that is missing here.

THE SENSE OF JUSTICE

Potter can do one of two things at this point. She can accommodate herself to what she takes to be Watson's injustice, or she can impose upon him to redress the wrong. Suppose she opts for the first alternative, deciding to swallow her pride and accept the apparent violation of her rights by the obtuse, insensitive, inconsiderate Watson. Perhaps her interests are not really that important and Watson's transgressions not that serious. Perhaps there are more pressing demands on her time and energy, or perhaps the costs of getting Watson to acknowledge her claim of right are simply beyond her means. Although many might choose to take this route, abject capitulation cannot and should not be the general response to obvious violations of right. It cannot because of the often observed human predilection to respond strongly and indignantly to injustice, to protest violations of rights, not only when we are the victims but as well when others are victimized. Potter's sense of injustice may have been aroused, and in this she may not be alone. About this "sense of injustice" Edmond Cahn has written:

> Among its facets are the demands for equality, desert, human dignity, conscientious adjudication, confinement of government to its proper functions and fulfillment of common expectations. . . . It denotes that sympathetic reaction of outrage, horror, shock, resentment and anger, those affections of the viscera and abnormal secretions of the adrenals that prepare the human animal to resist attack. Nature has thus equipped all men to regard injustice to another as personal aggression. Through a mysterious and magical *empathy*

or imaginative interchange, each projects himself into the shoes of the other, not in pity or compassion merely, but in the vigor of self-defense. Injustice is transmuted into assault; the sense of injustice is the implement by which assault is discerned and defense is prepared.

Justice thus acquires its public meaning, those in a given ethos perceive the same threat and experience the same organic reactions. It is possible to speak of injustice without utter relativism or solipsism, just because of this astonishing interchangeability within man's imagination. If a man did not have the capacity to recognize oppression of another as a species of attack upon himself, he would be unready—in a glandular sense—to face the requirements of juridic survival. In fine, the human animal is predisposed to fight injustice.[3]

If Cahn is correct, it may be unreasonable to expect Potter, and others comparably angered by what they take to be injustice, to accept whatever indignities are being meted out. Human beings are not so constituted.

But if it were open to us to craft our character and bring ourselves to the point where we could accept injustice—where we could abide it without struggle—would it be wise in that case to do so? At least two lines of thought lead to the conclusion that it would not. In the first place, a world in which the unjust could act with complete impunity would likely be an unjust world. As Thrasymachus reminds us at the beginning of Plato's *Republic,* there are surely many who would feel free to violate the rights of others if they thought they could get away with it. Thus passive acceptance of injustice would likely lead to a world characterized by more violations of important rights than people have to tolerate. And so it would seem to make sense, in general, actively to defend one's rights against violation. As Edmund Burke is widely supposed to have said, "The only thing necessary for the triumph of evil is for good men to do nothing."

But suppose one were willing to accept the consequences of living in a world in which no effort was made to require people to take into account the rights of others. Although it might be imprudent, is it actually wrong to be so willing to allow one's rights to be violated? In an article entitled "Servility and Self-Respect," Thomas E. Hill, Jr., argues that it is.

> . . . One must, so to speak, take up the spirit of morality as well as meet the letter of its requirements. To keep one's promises, avoid hurting others, and the like, is not sufficient; one should also take an attitude of respect towards the principles, ideals, and goals of morality. A respectful attitude towards a system of rights and duties consists of more than a disposition to conform to its definite rules of behavior; it also involves holding the system in esteem, being unwilling to ridicule it, and *being reluctant to give up one's place in it* [emphasis added]. . . . A person who fully respected a system of moral rights would be disposed to learn his proper place in it, to affirm it proudly, and not to tolerate abuses of it lightly.[4]

[3] *The Sense of Injustice* (Bloomington: Indiana University Press, 1949), pp. 22–25.
[4] *The Monist,* 57 (January 1973): 99.

Perhaps, then, Potter ought to do something. But whatever she decides to do to secure her claim of right, it will have to be done without Watson's cooperation. In his opinion he has not violated any of Potter's rights and thus her claim against him is without merit; there is no point in further consideration of the matter. Under the circumstances, whatever measures Potter decides to take in order to redress her grievance will have to be *imposed* upon Watson.

In considering Watson's options, it is fitting to begin with what might be called "vendetta culture" and the problems with it that John Locke has developed in *The Second Treatise of Government*. Locke considers that human actions may transgress law even prior to the origin of the state. Since in this "state of nature" there is no government to which one can appeal when one's rights are violated, one is permitted in these circumstances to take matters into one's own hands. (Indeed, prior to the state, there are no other hands in which these matters properly belong.) As Locke puts it:

> In transgressing the Law of Nature, the Offender declares himself to live by another Rule, than that of *reason* and common Equity . . . and so he becomes dangerous to Mankind, the tye, which is to secure them from injury and violence, being slighted and broken by him. Which being a trespass against the whole Species, and the Peace and Safety of it, provided for by the Law of Nature, every man upon this score, by the right he hath to preserve Mankind in general, may restrain, or where it is necessary, destroy things noxious to them, and so may bring such evil on any one, who hath transgressed that Law, as may make him repent the doing of it, and thereby deter him, and by his Example, others, from doing the like mischief. And in this case, and upon this ground, every *Man hath a Right to punish the Offender, and be Executioner of the Law of Nature.*
>
> (*Second Treatise*, Sec. 8)

Be aware that what Locke describes is not a semimythical, prehistoric tableau. Where one cannot make an appeal to a sufficiently respected and powerful authority, the vendetta may be the expected—and, arguably, the proper—response to wrongdoing, especially when the bonds of cooperation and reciprocity have been dissolved. Two examples should suffice to make the point. The complaints of juveniles against other juveniles frequently are not taken seriously by those in authority. Moreover, those in authority often lack the respect of juveniles. Thus it is not surprising that "getting even," alone or in concert with others, is a vivid feature of many childhoods. The teenage gang, or something like it, is precisely what one would expect to emerge within vendetta culture, offering, as it does, a vastly increased capacity for retaliation against outsiders. Prisons provide a second striking example. In practice, prison inmates cannot always appeal to those in authority when their rights are violated by other prisoners. Jack Henry Abbott, writing from prison, has observed:

> There is a boundary in each man. He can bend, sure. He can eat crow, and brown-nose to an extent. He can shuck the man for a while, become a good

actor. But when a man goes beyond that last essential boundary, it alters his ontology, so to speak. It's like the small pebble that starts a landslide no one can stop. You can betray others until, lo, you've betrayed yourself. . . .

Most convicts don't cross that line. You accept violence, committing it to survive morally as well as biologically. You're not a "psycho" or a killer—but that doesn't mean you won't kill and commit mind-boggling acts of violence. It is terribly hard to bring yourself to these acts, but you take a deep breath, look intelligently at what you must do and do it, even though you are scared stiff and sick to your stomach. It is something a man has to do sometimes.[5]

Locke was well aware of the problems with "street justice." In the *Second Treatise* he sketches what have become standard criticisms.[6] First, since persons generally do not study and reflect about issues involving justice, there is rarely a settled and understood standard for the resolution of disputes. Accordingly, individual efforts to secure justice are very likely to be injustices themselves (Sec. 124). Second, because persons are generally biased in favor of their own interests and those of their friends—especially so in the heat of conflict—they will tend to give themselves and their friends the benefit of the doubt in determining both the standards that should govern the settlement of disputes and the facts to which the standards apply. Thus, as with the preceding criticism, the attempt to secure justice on one's own is likely rather to promote injustice (Secs. 13 and 125). Third, persons may be in the right in connection with some dispute and yet lack the power to secure that to which they are entitled. Likewise, they may be in the wrong and yet have the power to secure that to which they are not entitled (Sec. 126). Fourth and last—because of the variations in understanding and the human tendency toward bias—disputes, rather than being settled, will tend to be aggravated until they become full-scale feuds. Society will be preoccupied with an interminable succession of retaliatory acts. As Locke puts it, "nothing but confusion and disorder will follow . . ." (Sec. 13).

If it becomes necessary for Potter to act on her own or with the support of a few sympathetic friends, she may conclude that some kind of direct action is in order. She may consider tearing down the fence and threatening Watson with personal injury if he doesn't shape up. But in these cases Watson is not likely to appreciate the moral indignation expressed by Potter and her friends in their efforts at rectification. Indeed, what they take to be a straightforward attempt to secure justice, Watson is likely to see as vandalism and assault. And, far from settling the matter, Potter may have only further upset it. To her original dispute with Watson—over his right to build the fence—is added Watson's new dispute with Potter, over the destruction of his property and the threat of violence. The "confusion and disorder" of which Locke spoke will be compounded yet further when Watson arranges his retaliation.

If Locke is correct in his analysis of what he calls the "inconveniences" of vendetta culture, there are two good reasons for the community as a whole to take an interest in Potter's claim against Watson. First, each member of the community stands the chance of becoming embroiled in a dispute in which, in his or her judgment, the bounds of tolerability have been overstepped. In those cases in which a voluntary settlement between the parties cannot be reached, the community can further a common interest in justice (an interest shared by both Potter and Watson) by providing a mechanism for adjudication that is so devised as to make it *as likely as possible that the decision reached will be a just decision—both procedurally and substantively—and as likely as possible that it will be accepted as such by the parties to the dispute and by the community as a whole.* In standing by and enforcing the decisions that emerge from a sound adjudication procedure, the community can make it easier for its members to secure what they are entitled to without resort to direct action. Such a mechanism can represent a substantial improvement in the life of the community: The quality of relationships will depend less upon the relative power of those involved in the interaction and more upon responsible judgments concerning their rights. And second, even for those members of the community who are not directly involved in disputes with others, it cannot be pleasant to live in a community that is wracked by incessant feuds. If instituting a mechanism for the adjudication of disputes can serve to secure more of the blessings of peace, that too is a reason for going ahead with it.[7]

THE THEORY OF ADJUDICATION

At its most basic level, the social choice to deal with disputes through adjudication secures for members of the community four distinctive rights. First, it secures the right to submit certain types of complaint to a judge or a tribunal. Second, it secures for the complaining party (we will henceforth use the legal term "plaintiff") the right to have the other party to the dispute (the "defendant") summoned to the court to answer the charges made in the complaint. Third, the judge having heard and considered the claims and arguments of both sides, it secures the right to have the judge make a decision in the case. And fourth, if the decision is in favor of the plaintiff, it secures for the plaintiff the right to have the judge's decision enforced against the defendant. As with direct action, adjudication is imposed on the offending party: There is no need for the plaintiff to persuade the defendant to submit to it. But unlike direct action, the impositions are made not by the aggrieved party in the dispute but by persons who have been given their authority (their special permission to act on behalf of others) by the community as a whole.

It is not difficult to see how the setting up of a court system can help the community overcome the Lockean inconveniences of vendetta culture.

---

[7] It may be that Locke is not correct in his assessment of vendetta culture. Political theorists in the communitarian anarchist tradition have argued that people are more disposed to cooperation than Locke supposed. And libertarians have suggested that the evils of vendetta culture and its variants may be less serious than those of the alternatives that are usually considered: Though the disease of vendetta culture may be bad, the cure may be worse.

Standards

Since judges have special responsibilities to decide questions of justice, they can be expected to reflect extensively upon these matters. Given an issue, if it is possible at all to make a responsible judgment on it—that is to say a judgment that takes into account the relevant available evidence and arguments—it is more likely that this can be done if someone is designated as having primary responsibility in such matters. While a responsible judgment can, of course, be wrong, it is less likely to be so than one that is uninformed and ill-considered. Thus the designation of judges who are expected to study and reflect upon the requirements of justice may be part of a better way to achieve a settled and understood standard for the resolution of disputes. Adjudication provides more grounds for hope than does vendetta culture.

Bias

Except where the judge is personally involved in the dispute or closely associated with one of the disputants, he or she is more likely to be able to approach the issue in the case in a disinterested way. Of course a judge might have a personal stake in the question to be resolved and thus might be expected to decide the issue either out of self-interest or so to avoid the appearance of bias. But even that problem can be solved if judges routinely refrain from participating in cases where such a problem might arise.[8]

Power

In agreeing to stand behind the decision of the court, the community does much to equalize the power of the parties. Thus differences in the power to enforce a judgment need not create differences in the ability to obtain justice. This can be an important advantage of adjudication.

Feuds

Where the decision of a judge is a responsible one, taking into account available and relevant evidence and arguments; where it is plainly free from the taint of bias; and where the community as a whole stands behind it, the parties to the dispute are very likely to accept the matter as settled. It is one thing to contest a decision by a neighbor; it is quite another to rail against one's whole community. Indeed, when those involved in the court system do their work well and the decisions of the courts are respected, there is likely to be very little need for actual enforcement. Nearly everyone will voluntarily comply with court orders and the law, not, in gen-

---

[8] The American Bar Association Code of Judicial Conduct provides, under Canon 3, that "A judge should disqualify himself in a proceeding in which his impartiality might reasonably be questioned. . . ."

eral, because they fear the power of the state, but because they can appreciate the reasonableness of the law's requirement.[9]

Given that the community has made a decision to provide a mechanism for adjudication, two fundamental questions remain regarding the general nature of that mechanism. First, what is to be the relationship between the courts and the means by which the community hammers out its public arrangements for cooperation (its mechanism for legislation)? Second, what are to be the basic responsibilities of the adjudicator? The answers to these questions will greatly affect the nature of the court system and, in consequence, the duties of those with offices within it.

JUDICIAL INDEPENDENCE

Let us assume that our community has reached a size at which it can no longer manage its problems in meetings of the general membership, and that, as a consequence, procedures have been devised for the election of representatives to a body that will address the common concerns of the community. The community gives this legislative body special permission (authority) to pursue a carefully specified set of purposes on its behalf but at the same time denies it the authority to pursue certain other purposes or to use certain means in the furtherance of authorized purposes. For example, the legislature may be permitted to enact legislation promoting the general welfare but explicitly denied the authority to set up a state religion. Thus, even if all the legislators believe that the general welfare might best be promoted by establishing a state religion, the legislature may not set it up, because it has been denied the authority to do so. Setting up a state religion is among those things the legislature has not been permitted to do. The legislature will thus have only *limited authority* to attend to the community's concerns.

Because the notion of limited authority is highly important[10] in legal work but not very well understood in other contexts, it is appropriate to consider it with some care. For clarity, one might think of the limited authority that teachers have. An English teacher may require that, on pain of failing the course, students write

---

[9] This will not be so in revolutionary political contexts where what is in question is the permission the courts claim to make decisions on behalf of the community. Revolutionaries may claim either that the courts do not have this authority, or that, although they have it, it ought to be revoked. In either event those in the judicial system may have partially or completely lost the respect they need in order for the courts to function. Adjudication cannot succeed in averting open conflict when what is at issue is the prevailing mechanism of adjudication itself.

[10] ". . . [T]here emerges in most systems a general rule that declares that top authority has only those powers explicitly granted. . . . The contemporary common rule—that authority be specific—that A exercise authority over B only in specified circumstances for a specific category of responses—man can claim as one of his great inventions. Although its origins are lost in a distant past, its restatement and refinement are recorded from time to time, as in the Magna Carta. However commonplace today, the rule is an historical development of the first order of importance." Charles A. Lindblom, *Politics and Markets* (New York: Basic Books, Inc., 1977), pp. 127–28.

papers and take examinations. But he would not have the authority to require that they clean up his backyard. Of course he could say he is requiring it. But this would be to appeal to powers that have not been accorded to him: *ultra vires,* in the language of the law. An *ultra vires* enactment is a nullity: Students would not be obligated to clean up the backyard despite the instructor's announced "requirement." The test for whether an enactment is *ultra vires* involves reference to the purposes and constraints of the office. For a teacher of English, course requirements must somehow further student mastery of the subject; cleaning up a backyard is clearly not a means to this end. And not every means is permitted. Teachers may not levy fines on slow learners. For a legislature, the purposes and constraints might be given at the time of its constitution. Of course, while clearly there are limits to the authority of teachers, students may not have available to them the means to ensure that these limits are observed. It is one thing to have the right not to have to clean up your teacher's backyard. It is quite another to have that right secured.

Within the limits set in its constitution, the legislature has the authority—indeed, the responsibility—to give effect somehow to the various purposes and goals that are articulated in the political process. Elected legislators are accountable to their constituents and must reconcile their official behavior with the judgment of the electorate. The legislative process itself involves negotiation and reasoned discussion as legislators with different constituencies endeavor to do their best for the people they serve. As policies emerge from this process and as statutes implementing them are enacted, the interests of some members of the community may be secured as legal rights, whereas the rights of other members may be extinguished. For example, the legislature may determine that, because of an oil shortage, people should be encouraged to install solar water heaters. They might implement this decision by prohibiting the construction of anything that would throw a solar energy collector into the shadow. Thus those who install solar water heaters will obtain a legislatively secured right that the sunlight not be blocked from falling upon the devices. Those who might otherwise have built structures obstructing this light will lose the legal right to do so. Thus in furthering the purposes of the community, the legislature both creates and extinguishes legal rights.

One might conclude that, since the legislature is in the business of securing rights anyway, why not let them act as the court system as well? Couldn't cases like *Potter* v. *Watson* be referred to the legislature for disposition? Or if, as is likely, the legislature was simply too busy with other things to handle all of the cases that would arise, couldn't the legislature appoint a deputy to issue decisions on its behalf? In some cases the legislature may already have passed statutes which clearly settle the issue in dispute. And in these cases the deputy has merely to declare the law. But in other cases the language used in legislation may be unclear, statutes may conflict with one another, or the legislature may have been silent on the matter. Here deputies will fill the gaps left by the legislature, acting in accordance with their best judgment about how the community's interests are to be served. It may seem then that a judge is best conceived as a kind of deputy legislature, carrying out a lawmaking function where the legislative process has left matters unsettled. While judges must defer to statutes enacted by the legislature, they are free to "fill the interstices" with legislation of their own choosing. A judicial decision is thus like a legislative enactment of a statute.[11]

But there are good reasons for rejecting this account of the operation of the courts. To begin with, one should note that there are two distinct ways in which a right can be secured: legislatively and judicially. In the first, one succeeds in persuading the community to adopt some social arrangement in the context of which the right is *created*. In the second, one succeeds in establishing that one has a right that ought to be *recognized*. In the first case a new right comes into existence through legislation; in the second, a right is acknowledged by the court.

Consider what it would be like if, instead of taking Watson to court, Potter went to the legislature (or to its deputy) and persuaded them to pass a law prohibiting the construction of fences like Watson's. Such a law would serve to create a legislatively secured right for Potter that Watson not build his fence. It would, accordingly, extinguish whatever right Watson had to build it. But in our case Watson has already completed the construction of his fence by the time the law is passed. And at the time he built it, he had the legal right to do so. While a legislature has the authority to create rights through the enactment of statutes, it seems it should not be granted the authority to extinguish rights retroactively, to enact *ex post facto* laws. For if it had this power, it would not be possible to conform one's actions to law since applicable laws might not have existed at the time of the action. The legislature could pass laws falsifying any legal judgment whatever. Moreover, it would not be fair to hold persons to legal standards that did not exist in any sense at the time of their actions. Thus if Watson has a right not to be subject to *ex post facto* laws, Potter's appeal to the legislature, however successful she is in convincing them, cannot establish that Watson lacked the right to build his fence. The legislature can act to extinguish his right, but it cannot properly bring it about that he never had that right.

In fact, as we have presented the case, neither Potter nor Watson is urging a change in the system of laws determining property rights. Both are claiming that their rights to their property justify their claims. Under adjudication, the judge endeavors to decide which of the two is correct. Once the judge does this, the law is settled. The community will recognize and enforce the claim of one or the other. The clarification that judicial decisions bring to law is not the same as the effect of *ex post facto* laws. The practice of passing *ex post facto* laws can leave every legal matter unsettled. But the practice of deciding contested legal issues in the courts

---

[11] This is, in fact, a widely held view of the judicial process. One finds statements of it in the legal realist tradition (see Jerome Frank's *Courts on Trial*) and in the legal positivist tradition (see H. L. A. Hart's *The Concept of Law*). The view developed here, however, is one that has recently supplanted the realist-positivist concept of the role of the judge. It has been persuasively set out by Ronald Dworkin in his *Taking Rights Seriously* (Cambridge: Harvard University Press, 1977), especially Chapter 4 ("Hard Cases"), and by Theodore Benditt in his *Law as Rule and Principle* (Stanford: Stanford University Press, 1978). Much of my discussion here is drawn from these two works.

can conduce to greater clarity. The way in which the courts secure rights is thus very different from the way in which legislatures do it.

There are two other reasons for distinguishing the legislative process from the judicial. First, the election of representatives gives some legitimacy, in terms of democratic theory, to statutes passed by the legislature. When legislators take their responsibilities seriously, the political process gives us reason to believe that the puposes being furthered by statutes are reflective of the purposes of the public. Representatives are accountable to those who elect them and are participants in the discussions and negotiations that lead to the passage of the legislation. But though we may not always be satisfied with this process, it is far more likely to result in equitable decisions than is the practice of allowing a lone judge, not responsible to a public constituency, to determine both the goals of the public and the means by which they are to be achieved. As Dworkin puts it, representative democracy "works better than a system that allows nonelected judges, who have no mail bag or lobbyists or pressure groups, to compromise competing interests in their chambers."[12] But the designation of an independent impartial judge does make sense if the purpose of the office is simply to assess the arguments and claims of those embroiled in conflict.

The second reason involves the limited authority of the legislature. We must ask whether members of the community should have legal recourse against the legislature—the right to challenge it in court—if in their judgment the legislature has exceeded its authority. If the court system *is* the legislature (or some extension of it), then the "court" clearly cannot be taken to be unbiased in such cases. The defendant in this type of case would be the "judge." The legislature cannot be expected to assess impartially the claim that its own enactments are *ultra vires* and should therefore be nullified. If citizens are to have rights against the community and these rights are to be secured—if they are not mere window dressing—then the judicial system must be separate from the legislature.

JUDICIAL RESPONSIBILITY

Given that the community has decided to set up an independent judiciary, it must select judges and decide what responsibilities they will assume. We shall not explore the question of how the community will designate judges but only note that it cannot choose them on the basis of its idea of the substantive decisions they are likely to make. When candidates for judicial office announce their predilections or when they are selected because they are believed to have certain leanings, judges cannot be expected to decide cases impartially. People will have good reason to believe that these judges have already made up their minds on matters to be argued before the court and that they will not give opposing views a fair hearing. Judicial decisions will therefore be less likely to settle disputes. However it decides to select judges,

[12] Dworkin, *Taking Rights Seriously,* p. 85.

the community will have to do so in a way that respects the need for impartiality as a part of the integrity of the judicial system.

The second issue, concerning the determination of judicial responsibility, can be taken up in three parts. First, shall primary responsibility for conducting the investigation fall on the parties to the dispute, or shall the judge be charged with this responsibility? This question requires the community to choose between an inquisitorial and an adversarial process of adjudication. Second, shall the judge's decision apply only to the case before the court, or shall the judge declare a rule applying to all relevantly similar cases? This question requires the community to decide whether the judicial system will incorporate the doctrine of precedent. Lastly, shall the judge in each case simply issue a decision, or must that decision be accompanied by its justification? The question here involves judicial accountability. The resolution of each of these matters may have consequences of great moment. We will take up each issue separately.

The first one concerns the responsibility for conducting the investigation. Historically, two models of adjudication have been used: adversarial and inquisitorial. In an adversarial system the basic responsibility for gathering evidence and marshaling arguments belongs to the parties to the dispute. The judge merely listens to the presentations of both sides, generally without taking an active role in developing the evidence or arguments. Judicial responsibility here consists solely in the creation of a forum in which the parties to the dispute can argue their cases, presenting the law and the facts as they see them. After the parties have been heard, the judge makes a decision, taking into account what has been submitted to the court. By contrast, in an inquisitorial system, the basic responsibility for gathering evidence and marshaling arguments belongs to the adjudicator. The judge, sometimes with the help of an investigating magistrate, conducts an inquiry into the facts and the law and develops a judgment largely on his or her own initiative. The parties to the dispute are not expected to assume responsibility for the discovery of relevant evidence or applicable lines of legal reasoning.

Adversarial systems have the potentially serious disadvantage that cases may be wrongly decided if the party in the right loses because he or she is unable to present intelligibly and persuasively what is, in fact, a solid case. Since the judge in an adversarial proceeding depends on the contesting parties to do the investigative work and to present the results to the court in a useful way, cases may be wrongly decided if one of the parties is unable to meet these two requirements of adversarial adjudication. Indeed, cases may not be brought to court in the first place if an injured party fears that he or she cannot meet the requirements. When this happens, we are back almost to the inconveniences of vendetta culture—not completely, however, because the party doing the injuring may actually be protected by the law in a way that his victim is not. Thus in these cases the judicial system may serve generally to protect perpetrators of injustice; may serve, in other words, to further injustice. The inquisitorial system would appear not to have these problems, since one individual is doing the investigating for both sides. Injustice stemming from inequality in the resources of the parties is thus less likely to occur. If the community opts for an adversarial model, it will have to address that model's distinctive problem. Although more will be said about this problem later on, here it will be noted that its solution can involve a professionalized community of attorneys serving as the intermediary between a lay public and a legal system requiring specialized knowledge and skill.

The inquisitorial model is not free from difficulties either. Lon L. Fuller and John D. Randall have set forth what they take to be the most serious problems arising when a judge attempts to decide a case without "partisan advocacy."

> What generally occurs in practice is that at some early point a familiar pattern will seem to emerge from the evidence; an accustomed label is waiting for the case and, without awaiting further proofs, this label is promptly assigned to it. It is a mistake to suppose that this premature cataloguing must necessarily result from impatience, prejudice or mental sloth. Often it proceeds from a very understandable desire to bring the hearing into some order and coherence, for without some tentative theory of the case there is no standard of relevance by which testimony may be measured. But what starts as a preliminary diagnosis designed to direct inquiry tends, quickly and imperceptibly, to become a fixed conclusion as all that confirms the diagnosis makes a strong imprint on the mind while all that runs counter to it is received with diverted attention.
>
> An adversary presentation seems the only effective means for combatting this natural human tendency to judge too swiftly in terms of the familiar that which is not yet fully known. The arguments . . . hold the case, as it were, in suspension between two opposing interpretations of it. While the proper classification of the case is thus kept unresolved, there is time to explore all of its peculiarities and nuances.[13]

If Fuller and Randall are right, it is the adversary system that is more likely to guarantee that a party to a dispute will be heard. Unlike the judge in an inquisitorial system, the judge in an adversarial system need not begin the task of forming a judgment until after the evidence and arguments have been presented. But of course, as we noted, something must be done to help those who are unable to meet the requirements of adversarial adjudication.

The second issue that the community must settle concerns the doctrine of precedent. When a decision is issued in a particular case, does the judge's authority cover only the case at hand, or does the rule that the judge articulates apply to any similar case arising in the community? Consider what it would be like to opt for the first arrangement. Suppose, several years before *Potter* v. *Watson,* Cotter and Matson had brought a similar dispute to the court. Suppose in that earlier case the court had recognized Matson's right to build his fence without having to take into account Cotter's interests (interests having the same general character as Potter's later on). Though the arguments that persuaded the judge in *Cotter* v. *Matson* might be interesting to the judge in *Potter* v. *Watson,* the fact that the earlier judge decided in favor of Matson would not, in and of itself, be relevant. Even though the community as a whole, through the judge in *Cotter* v. *Matson,* had recognized Matson's right to build his fence, the decision the judge made then pertained only to that case. It did not apply to any other, regardless of how great the similarity.

---

[13] "Professional Responsibility: Report of the Joint Conference," 44 *A.B.A.J.* 1159 (1958).

In Chinese legal thought, there is a long tradition of opposition to precedent as we understand it and, even more broadly, opposition to the very idea of written legal rules. By the fifth century B.C. and in Confucianism as it prevailed for over 2,000 years in the Chinese legal system, judicial decisions were widely considered properly to be grounded in the estimable cultivation of the judge's character rather than in the rules of law to be found in codes and earlier decisions. In a well-known letter written about 2,500 years ago, a Chinese dignitary complained thus to the prime minister of a neighboring state:

> Originally, sir, I had hope in you, but now that is all over. Anciently, the early kings conducted their administration by deliberating on matters [as they arose]; they did not put their punishments and penalties [into writing], fearing that this would create a contentiousness among the people which could not be checked. Therefore they used the principle of social rightness to keep the people in bounds, held them together through their administrative procedures, activated for them the accepted ways of behavior, maintained good faith toward them, and presented them with [examples of] benevolence. . . .
>
> But when the people know what the penalties are, they lose their fear of authority and acquire a contentiousness which causes them to make their appeal to the written word [of the penal laws], on the chance that this will bring them success [in court cases]. . . . As soon as the people know the grounds on which to conduct disputation, they will reject the [unwritten] accepted ways of behavior and make their appeal to the written word, arguing to the last over the tip of an awl or knife. Disorderly litigations will multiply. . . .[14]

There may well be contexts in which it makes good sense not to use decisions in earlier cases as the basis for deciding later ones. Arbitrators, who work for the disputants themselves (not for the community), are not bound to take into account the decisions of earlier arbitrators. And the World Court at The Hague does not use the doctrine of precedent in issuing decisions in disputes involving nations. But if Watson were to lose his case after Matson had won his earlier, if the community had recognized a right for Matson that it refused to acknowledge for Watson, if it had done this without showing that the two cases were really not the same or that the earlier case was wrongly decided, Watson might well have a persuasive claim that he was being treated unequally, unfairly and unjustly.[15]

Moreover, if earlier decisions have not settled the law but only the dispute, they cannot be used in efforts to determine what the law has to say on particular matters. In endeavoring to hold one's activities within the bounds of legality, there would be no reason to rely on what the courts have had to say. For these reasons,

---

[14] James Legge, tr, *The Chinese Classics*, Vol. V (Hong Kong: Hong Kong University Press, 1960), p. 609; modified by D. Bodde and quoted in Derk Bodde and Clarence Morris, *Law in Imperial China* (Philadelphia: University of Pennsylvania Press, 1967), pp. 16–17.

[15] A frequently given account of justice holds that it involves treating similar cases similarly. To be sure, much more needs to be said about justice than this. Nonetheless, it appears that injustices are frequently a consequence of such unequal treatment. If Bender and Harter both receive scores of 85 on a test, the instructor acts unjustly if she gives one an A and the other a C. See, for example, Chapter 7 of Joel Feinberg's *Social Philosophy* (Englewood Cliffs: Prentice-Hall, Inc., 1973).

it has generally been held that courts ought to hand down rulings that apply not only in the cases presented but also in any comparable disputes that may later arise. And the law having been declared for the community, other judges should be required to follow and apply the rulings unless they can show either that the case coming before them is distinguishable from the earlier one or that the earlier case was wrongly decided. Needless to say, they must be very careful about how often they do the latter, since if judges continually declare themselves in error, they will not succeed in settling the law. More to the point, they should take great pains to ensure that their judgments are correct, since it will always be costly to correct the effects of judicial negligence.

The third issue that the community must settle concerns whether the judge shall simply issue a decision in a case or whether that decision shall be accompanied by the judge's justification. If the judge is not accountable in this way, not required publicly to justify the decision, it will not be possible to criticize judicial action on the grounds that the judge's reasoning was faulty or that irrelevant or false propositions were determinative of the decision. One might think that the harder it is to criticize a judicial decision, the better the judicial system will function; people will go along with decisions, not because they accept the soundness of the supporting considerations (they won't know what these are), but rather because they respect the office of the judge. One is less likely to criticize an office than to object to the reasons given by an office holder. The French judicial system works this way, without public justification for particular judicial decisions.[16]

But the withholding of the judge's reasons may well breed distrust in the system itself. Parties to the dispute have no assurance that their arguments have been heard and understood, and the community cannot be sure that relevant considerations not raised by the parties have been taken into account. To be sure, the requirement that the judge provide a justification for a decision does make the office a more burdensome one. But if judges are conscientious in arriving at decisions, replying to arguments made in court and ensuring that relevant considerations not raised by the parties are given due attention,[17] it should not be difficult—indeed it should be helpful—to organize the favored line of argument in a prepared document.

---

[16] On the French judicial system see Gray Dorsey, "Legal Ethics and the Adversary System," in Paul Kurtz and others, eds., *Ethics in Teaching and Scientific Research* (Buffalo: Prometheus Books, 1977), pp. 99–115.

[17] This point does set a limit to the nonparticipation of judges in adversarial proceedings. While a judge does not have primary responsibility for developing relevant lines of argument, he or she is not obligated to ignore all considerations not raised by the parties. If the decision in the case only affected the parties to the dispute, judges might confine their analyses solely to the arguments submitted. But since the rule the judge articulates applies to the community as a whole, the judge's responsibility would seem to require an active role where the parties have left important stones unturned. One advantage of the adversary system would seem to be its ability to become more like an inquisitorial system when the attorneys involved are unable or unwilling to develop applicable lines of argument. Of course, in general, where the judge does uncover some new aspect of the case, that approach should be made known to the disputants for reply before the final judgment is reached. During the Watergate trials Judge John Sirica incorporated in his court elements of a more inquisitorial approach under circumstances in which the prosecution could not be counted on to press its case.

Moreover, the requirement of public justification can serve as a reminder to judges that certain reasons are improper. For example, the judge in *Potter* v. *Watson* could hardly give as a reason for finding in favor of Watson that he is her son-in-law. The discipline of crafting judicial decisions that include a statement of the reasoning—especially where these are reviewable by higher courts in addition to the public—can underscore the requirement that judges not take into account, as part of their justification for official action, considerations that must be kept concealed.

But there is yet another reason for instituting this type of judicial accountability. As a body of opinions is developed, what will gradually become apparent is a certain manner in which judges approach questions of law, a distinct judicial intellectual posture. As long as judges communicate with one another about their work, this style will probably develop whether or not justifications are published. These specimens of specialized reasoning can be of as much value as the decisions themselves. In the first place they allow disputants to develop arguments in the manner that will be of greatest use to the courts. They can thus make the courts more efficient, permitting and encouraging litigants to do some of the work of the courts by casting arguments in the proper form. In the second place, an understanding of the manner in which judges assess a claim gives the potential litigant a sense of how a judge will evaluate the arguments that are likely to be advanced in court. A disputant—indeed both disputants—can make a good guess as to what the outcome of the case will be, even if earlier cases and statutes have left the issue unsettled. The practice of negotiating out-of-court settlements should not be seen as wholly separate from adjudication nor as a social alternative to it, for the negotiation of such settlements takes place against the background of the parties' expectations about the probable and possible outcomes of adjudication. These expectations can be better grounded if it is clear to the parties what judges are likely to say. Thus more cases may be settled out of court, and indeed disputes are less likely to arise, as the rationality of the courts becomes the rationality that the public employs in assessing the merits of claims of right. The judge, in stating the justification for a decision, is deferring to the authority of reason. The requirement that judges justify their decisions thus makes of the court not a forum in which one appeals to the person who holds the office of judge, but rather a forum in which one appeals to reason, or at least to that particular developed capacity for responsible judgment that should be the pride of the judiciary.

None of this is to say that the reasons given by the judge in an opinion are invariably or exclusively the reasons that decided the case. As with any position whatever, the office of judge may be corrupted or subverted by those who develop and conceal personal interests in cases or who follow hidden agendas. The appearance of judicial responsibility may be a sham and may conceal things mean and even sinister. Where this is generally so, it is hard to see what is gained by continuing community support of the court system. It is hard to see what is lost by exposing the lie. Such courts do not serve to rectify injustices but only perpetrate them on a larger scale. Against this background, vendetta culture and its variants can be refreshingly free of hypocrisy. In the end, a judicial system depends upon men and women who are committed to taking their responsibilities seriously and to seeing to it that other officers do so as well. If such trust in ourselves is misplaced, it bodes ill for all of us.

THE FUNCTIONS OF ATTORNEYS

While more will be said about complexity later on, here it will suffice to observe that, in a system of adjudication as sophisticated and complicated as ours, there will be few lay persons knowledgeable enough to be able to understand their legal situation when rights are contested or skilled enough to be able effectively to secure their rights, over the protestations of their adversaries, within the procedures established by the courts. When the legal system reaches a certain level of complexity, you will need expert assistance if you have business in court.

If Potter goes to an attorney for assistance in connection with her problem with Watson, there are two basic legal services she will probably seek: counseling and, if she decides to go forward, representation. In the first place she will want advice about her legal situation. What relevant rights does the law accord to property owners? What statutes or ordinances might be appealed to in seeking relief from Watson? What are the arguments that can be advanced on Potter's behalf? What counterarguments are available to Watson? What might it cost to secure relief? How long might it take? What measures might be required and what countermeasures might be provoked? What chance is there that Potter's cause will prevail in court? What could happen to Potter, psychologically, upon being swept up in litigation? What Potter needs is a good description of legal reality. She wants to make a decision about whether to pursue in the courts a resolution of her disagreement with Watson, and so she needs to know what is involved in that choice.

In counseling clients, a good lawyer will strive to be scrupulously realistic, trying not to give either an unduly pessimistic or overly optimistic picture of the way things are. Because so much can hang on the client's decision, attorneys will often need to research the issues before giving advice. What legal powers do others have the exercise of which might affect the client in significant ways: powers to arrest, to convict, to force disclosure, to tax, to seize, to sue, to enjoin, to revoke licenses or special privileges? The world view of a competent attorney seems characteristically to feature a strikingly heightened appreciation of hidden dangers, unsuspected liabilities, unsensed vulnerabilities. Among businesspersons, this professional gloom has given lawyers the reputation of being "deal killers." But beyond exposure to liability, clients may have powers and immunities that can serve to protect and further their interests. There may be procedures that can be undertaken on behalf of the client, procedures that can reduce legal exposure. In the course of competent counseling, the client's values, needs, interests, aspirations, desires, and concerns will emerge, and in the end some course of action will be chosen that ideally holds out the hope of maximizing the goods that the client wants to realize or protect while at the same time promising to minimize the evils that the client wants to diminish or avoid. Although advice may be given—"It appears to me that the wisest course of action would be to . . ."—the attorney must be careful not to impose his or her own values on the client. The criminal defendant may not wish to deny the charge. The spouse may not want to contest the inequitable property settlement. The corporation may be comfortable acting at a measured level of legal vulnerability. Counseling requires neutrality: The lawyer should acknowledge that it will be the client's values that must ultimately determine the course selected. (It is a separate question whether the attorney will assist the client in pursuing that course.) And counseling requires objectivity: The picture the lawyer paints of the world must not be colored to favor the course of action preferred by the lawyer. If there is a risk, it must be disclosed. If there is an option, the client must know about it.

But now suppose that Potter decides to seek redress through the courts. She retains the attorney and entrusts to him the matter of her dispute with Watson. He, the attorney, becomes her fiduciary. The second basic service provided by attorneys is that of representation. The shift from serving as a client's counselor to acting as his or her "zealous advocate" can be very striking. In contrast to the neutrality and objectivity of the counselor, an advocate functioning in the context of an adversarial proceeding is strongly partisan. A decision as to a course of action having been made, it will now be the client's interests that will inform the attorney's actions, coloring the way he represents the world and the law to the judge. The classic statement of the advocate's intellectual posture was given in 1820 by Henry (later Lord) Brougham in his defense of England's Queen Caroline against a charge of adultery brought by her husband, King George IV. Brougham knew—as many did—that there was such evidence of indiscretion on the King's part as could result in his forfeiture of the crown if the facts were to emerge at trial. As Brougham began his defense of Queen Caroline before the house of Lords, he reminded them

> that an advocate, in the discharge of his duty, knows but one person in all the world, and that person is his client. To save that client by all means and expedients, and at all hazards and costs to other persons and, amongst them, to himself, is his first and only duty; and in performing this duty he must not regard the alarm, the torments, the destruction which he may bring upon others. Separating the duty of a patriot from that of an advocate, he must go on reckless of consequences, though it should be his unhappy fate to involve his country in confusion.[18]

Three general observations need to be made about legal representation in an adversary system. In the first place, the attorney is the client's *agent*, and in turn the client is the attorney's *principal*. An important part of what this means is that, once the attorney is retained to represent a client in some matter, the actions of the attorney will characteristically be imputed to the client. If the lawyer settles, the client settles; if the lawyer loses, the client loses. Lawyers play with "other people's marbles." Accordingly, an important part of a competent attorney's job will be to work out with the client, carefully and fairly often, the precise authority that the

---

[18] 2 *Trial of Queen Caroline* 8 (1821).

client is giving over to the attorney. The task of educating the client—informing him or her of risks and options as these arise—may be an ongoing one as the case develops.

In the second place, the attorney is not an ordinary agent but, as noted earlier, a fiduciary. In the event of a dispute between attorney and client, the attorney will properly be held to a very high standard. To hold yourself out as an attorney is to represent yourself as having skill and dedication that go considerably beyond what ordinary persons are expected to display. Compare an agent who cares for the front yard of a homeowner with an agent who maintains a nuclear reactor for a power company. It is clear that there is an important public interest in ensuring that those who maintain nuclear plants adhere to the very highest standards in meeting their responsibilities. While we may not care if Mister Teller, across the street, hires a teenager to maintain his lawn—it is his bad luck if the grass dies—we would certainly take an interest if a public utility hired the same youth to keep its nuclear generator running. Professionals such as doctors and lawyers must be expected to exercise a quality of judgment that goes considerably beyond the ability of those who employ them. They must be expected as well to be scrupulously trustworthy and loyal to those who entrust concerns to them. The classic description of fiduciary obligation is given in *Meinhard* v. *Salmon.* It is a

> duty of the finest loyalty. Many forms of conduct permissible in the worka-day world for those acting at arm's length, are forbidden to those bound by fiduciary ties. A trustee is held to something stricter than the morals of the market place. Not honesty alone, but the punctilio of an honor the most sensitive, is then the standard of behavior. . . . [The fiduciary] had put himself in a position in which thought of self was to be renounced, however hard the abnegation. . . . For him and for those like him the rule of undivided loyalty is relentless and supreme.[19]

Without this confidence in the profession and its membership, the system of adjudication cannot do its job. Legal professionalism thus involves maintaining competence and attending to one's responsibilities to clients. It may be that drawing lines here—"Do I have the resources to take on this responsibility?" "Did I do everything I should have done for my client?" "Are there sufficient grounds to disbar this attorney for neglect or incompetence?"—is the most difficult problem in professional ethics.

Finally, *contra* Brougham, it must be noted that lawyers are more than the mere agents of their clients; attorneys are, essentially, officers of the court. In complicated legal systems, what attorneys may do on behalf of clients will be limited by the way in which their role fits into the adjudicatory procedures of the court. A lawyer is not a mere functionary, manipulated as a puppet by the whims of the client. There is a separate set of obligations to the court that must be honored if the system of adjudication is to serve its community. While the zealous furthering of the client's interests may be a paramount part of legal professionalism, that pursuit

---

[19] 164 N.E. 545, 546, 548 (1928).

must not compromise the integrity of the judicial system within which advocacy takes place. We would not want lawyers to bribe judges, threaten jurors with bodily harm, or fabricate false evidence. If one thinks seriously about the matter, it should become apparent that lawyers must not even speak privately to the judge without opposing counsel being present. It should be remembered that the purpose of the system of adjudication is to make it as likely as possible that the final decision will be a just decision—both procedurally and substantively—and that it will be accepted as such by the parties to the dispute and by the community as a whole. Much of what comes under the heading of professional responsibility represents constraints on zealous advocacy in the interests of "due process."

A special instance of just such a constraint applies to the prosecuting attorney in a criminal case. Until now we have been concerned with civil cases. Potter, the plaintiff, has her attorney and Watson, the defendant, has his. But now suppose that Potter, wholly unable to secure redress in the courts, shoots and kills Watson. Clearly the injured party, Watson, is no longer in a position to complain to the court about his neighbor's misdeed. Criminal law, which now comes into play, differs in important ways from civil. First, for some serious wrongdoings the community may not wish to rely on private attorneys, retained by those who are wronged, to pursue resolution of the matter through the courts. The community itself may choose to appropriate primary responsibility for the prosecution of such cases. Second, for very serious wrongdoings, rectification of the wrong and/or restitution—giving back the money that was stolen, paying for the treatment of the injuries that were maliciously inflicted—may not be sufficient. Beyond these requirements, there may be reasons to impose an officially administered punishment upon the wrongdoer, one that is in some way proportional to the seriousness of the wrongdoing or the culpability of the wrongdoer. Perhaps the punishment will educate the community as to what its standards are.[20] Perhaps punishment will deter prospective wrongdoers from similar criminality.[21] Perhaps the wrongdoer in some sense "deserves" the punishment.[22] Third and finally, because punishment for crime is the most burdensome imposition that a community can visit upon one of its members, we may wish to design the criminal justice system in such a way as to make it unlikely that innocent persons will be convicted. If the system fails, it will fail safely, without punishing an innocent person. In contrast, in a civil case the finder of fact must judge on the basis of which side has the weightier evidence (the "preponderance of the evidence" test): The plaintiff's attorney need only build a better case than the defendant's attorney. But the attorney for the state in a criminal prosecution must do more than that. The burden is on the prosecution to prove that the accused is guilty "beyond a reasonable doubt." The defendant's attorney need only create a reasonable doubt.

[20] Jean Hampton, "The Moral Education Theory of Punishment," *Philosophy and Public Affairs* 13 (1984): 208–38.

[21] See, for example, Steven Goldberg, "On Capital Punishment," *Ethics* 85 (1974): 67–74.

[22] Herbert Morris, "Persons and Punishment," *The Monist* 52 (1968): 475–501.

In serving the community, the prosecuting attorney pursues the community's interest in justice. It must not be the purpose of the office to convict the accused, for the accused may not be guilty, and the community has no interest in punishing the innocent. Thus, for example, when evidence emerges that is favorable to the defendant, the prosecution must make that evidence available to the other side. As we shall see in Chapter 4 in discussing confidentiality in criminal defense work, the same principle does not apply to the defendant's attorney.

OTHER LEGAL TASKS

Though counseling and representation may be the central responsibilities of the legal profession in sophisticated adversarial legal systems, it is almost inevitable that, as a consequence of their expertise, the profession will routinely take up other tasks as part of its work.

Chief among these is *negotiation.* Because taking a case to court—litigation—will generally be costly and because, as noted earlier, it will often be possible to antici- pate with some degree of accuracy the ultimate judgment of the court, it will often be rational for the parties to settle their dispute for what they expect the judge might award them, discounted by (1) the probability that they might lose and by (2) the costs incurred in litigation. Negotiation raises many ethical problems. In practice it may favor—like poker, for example—those who can successfully dissimu- late. Negotiators will gain the advantage if they can persuade their counterparts that they will prevail in court because no expense will be spared in pursuing the cause. This proposition may not be true, of course. Still, it may not be necessary to tell outright lies in order to create the desired false belief. It is possible to become adept in the art of misleading others without ever uttering an untruth. While one might deplore the cheapening of the spoken word in such discourse, one might reason that not much harm need be done if trained lawyers all play the same game, huffing and puffing in the same way. They will all simply discount the standard exaggeration factor; and, except for some who are new to the game, no one will be fooled. But then if no one gets fooled, one may wonder why discourse in legal negotiations needs to sink to such a low standard. Ethical problems in negotiations are not unique to the legal profession; they are quite common in business, for example.[23]

Because attorneys have developed a sensitivity to the perils implicit in the exer- cise of certain legal powers—forming a partnership, selling real estate, writing a will, coming to an enforceable agreement, registering a patent—they are frequently in- volved in *nonadversarial representation.* While there is always a possibility that ad- versariness may erupt afterwards, skilled legal assistance can help the client to achieve ends in such a way as to eliminate or diminish grounds for complaint that could create conflict later on. A well-prepared contract will clarify in advance the

---

[23] Sissela Bok, *Lying: Moral Choice in Public and Private Life* (New York: Pantheon Books, Inc., 1978).

terms of cooperation. A well-drafted will can clearly document the substance of that important decision. A patent application may be drafted in such a way as to make it very difficult for others to reap where your client has sown. Typically such tasks involve the preparation of papers that, for example, give effect to decisions, document events, petition for the granting of legal privileges, or memorialize the terms of cooperation.

In all of these tasks, there must be a relationship of trust and confidence between the attorney and the client. The ethical problems of the legal profession overwhelmingly require a subtle understanding and appreciation of trust and multiple responsibilities. It is to some of these problems that we now turn.

Chapter 3

Conflict of Interest
and Conflict of Obligation

The term "conflict of interest" has its characteristic applications in settings in which formal responsibilities are assumed by individuals occupying certain more or less well-defined social roles. The notion is not well understood outside the legal profession, and even inside the profession it is probably not understood well enough. Part of the problem is that the expression itself is ambiguous, denoting at least two very different types of circumstance. Moreover, problems arising out of conflicts of interest are most obvious in formal types of relationship, such as that which obtains between lawyer and client. These have few counterparts in ordinary day-to-day life.

Our purposes here will be twofold. In the first place, we shall endeavor to distinguish among the different kinds of conflicts of interest. It is important not only for lawyers but for others as well—doctors, journalists, social workers—to be sensitive to the possibility that they may be involved in a conflict of interest. For this reason our discussion in what follows will utilize examples, where possible, not only from law but from other areas as well. In the second place, we shall attempt with respect to each of these types of conflict to isolate what it is exactly that makes the circumstance ethically interesting. Why should the ethically competent attorney be wary of conflict of interest? It is not enough to say, as many discussions of conflict of interest seem to, that you or your client may be caused to suffer for such inattention. That may be so, but the question still must be faced as to whether such penalties ought to be paid.

The two situations denoted by the term "conflict of interest" have very different ethical characteristics. Sometimes the concern is that an attorney either has or may come to have conflicting obligations. In other cases the concern is that some fact has called into question the loyalty of the attorney. Henceforth we will use the term "conflict of obligation" to refer to the first type of situation and will reserve the term "conflict of interest" exclusively for the second type. A third concept of conflict of interest has occasionally commanded the attention of philosophers. It obtains whenever there are two interests such that the satisfaction of either precludes the satisfaction of the other: One person may want the air conditioner on and another may want it off; or Jones may want the air conditioner on but may not be willing to pay the resulting electric bill. Although it will be important at points to note conflicts falling under this concept—we can call them "interests that are in conflict"—this notion will not be a central topic of this chapter.

CONFLICTS OF OBLIGATION:
ACTUAL AND POTENTIAL

Dexter, who used to box as a boy, has just started teaching his son and some of the youngsters from the neighborhood the basic elements of the sport. Working with heavily padded gloves, the boys have done well during several practice sessions and seem to be ready for their first matches. With Dexter serving as referee, the second bout begins with Dexter's son contending in the ring. Dexter tries to be fair as the two boys land punches on each other but nevertheless feels uncomfortable as he struggles to suppress any suggestion of favoritism toward his son. The match is a close one, and he wonders how the other boy will feel if he gives the bout to his son. He wonders how his son will feel if he gives the bout to the other boy. (Dexter's situation is reminiscent of one that befell a judge several hundred years ago. In the West of Ireland there is a memorial that tells the story. The judge had the misfortune to be on the bench when his son was brought before the court, accused, and found guilty of a capital offense. He resigned his position after sentencing his son to death.)

At the core of Dexter's uneasiness is an ethical dilemma that he has unwittingly brought upon himself. For Dexter is a father, and in at least one widespread view of that role, he has an obligation to be a partisan supporter of his young son. But Dexter is also the referee in a boxing match. As such his obligation is to be evenhanded and fair. Clearly there is nothing wrong with being a father, and clearly there is nothing wrong with being a referee. But there does seem to be something morally perilous about refereeing a match in which one's son is a contestant. With respect to one and the same youngster, Dexter must be both a partisan supporter and a disinterested judge; how can he meet either obligation without compromising his ability to fulfill the other? It is of little solace that there may be a right or a best answer to the dilemma: "If you have to decide between being a bad referee and a bad father, always choose . . ." Regardless of the answer, Dexter is in the unenviable position of having to decide what kind of creep he is going to be. The situation he has brought upon himself is one in which his obligations conflict with one another. Although the dilemma may be unresolvable once it has arisen, had he been sufficiently attentive to the ethical implications of the roles of father and referee, Dexter could have avoided the problem in the first place. For instance, he could have put off the boxing matches until he found someone else to referee them. But conflicts of obligation are not always that simple.

Flynn is driving along in her car with her two friends Chang and Ripley. Out of nowhere, a bus collides with her vehicle. Chang and Ripley are injured and require medical attention. While Flynn is not hurt, her car is damaged. A few weeks later the three meet with attorney Parker to discuss suing the bus company for damages.

The evidence supports the bus driver's being at fault, and Parker agrees to take the case. Chang's medical bills total $14,000; Ripley's, $3,000. Flynn's car requires $1,500 worth of repairs. Taking into account other costs to his clients, Parker files suit against the bus company for $25,000. As Parker has anticipated, the bus company files a countersuit against Flynn, claiming that the accident was her fault. At trial each side has the chance to present its case, and the jury is asked to decide who is at fault and how much each has to pay to whom. Horrified, Parker listens as the jury finds Flynn and the bus company equally at fault and equally liable for $17,000 in medical bills.[1]

Why is Parker horrified? If Flynn, the driver of the car, were Parker's sole client, Parker would be obligated to discuss with her the option of filing an appeal. There is a chance that Flynn could escape the $8,500 judgment against her and perhaps even recover the cost of repairing the car. Filing an appeal might be a very good idea. But if Chang and Ripley were Parker's only clients, suggesting an appeal would be absurd. They have essentially won their case. Merely to mention the word "appeal" to Flynn may be to betray Chang and Ripley. If Flynn decides to appeal, their award could be delayed for years. Conceivably, they might never receive payment. The authors of Canon 6 of the old A.B.A. Canons of Professional Ethics (superseded in 1970) had this situation in mind when they wrote that "a lawyer represents conflicting interests when, in behalf of one client, it is his duty to contend for that which duty to another client requires him to oppose." Parker has an obligation to Flynn to discuss with her the advisability of an appeal. And simultaneously he has an obligation to Chang and Ripley not to discuss with Flynn the advisability of an appeal. Parker is caught in a classic conflict of obligations.

But where exactly did Parker go wrong? We can appreciate, perhaps, that fathers should not referee boxing matches in which their sons are contenders. But what practical rule can attorneys adhere to that will serve to protect them against having to decide which client they are going to betray?

Without doubt, the most commonly given reply to our question is the injunction to be found in Matthew: "No man can serve two masters: for either he will hate the one, and love the other; or else he will hold to the one, and despise the other." While there may be wisdom in this New Testament language, it seems unlikely that Matthew's words can helpfully illuminate professional responsibility in law. In the first place, lawyers do not serve their clients as servants do their masters. For masters are owed obedience by those who serve them. Lawyers only rarely have obligations to obey their clients. For the most part, their service is autonomous. They are paid in order that they may do their work. In the second place, most practicing attorneys have no ethical problems in providing legal services for more than one client. If the Matthew rule were taken to be applicable to legal practice, it would entail the preposterous conclusion that no lawyer can have more than one client! While this would clearly reduce the incidence of conflicts of obligation in legal prac-

---

[1] The facts here are adapted from *Jedwabney* v. *Philadelphia Transportation Company*, 390 PA 231, 135 A.2d 252 (1957).

tice, it is hardly a suggestion that any attorney would take seriously. In this situation, Parker could not even decide to represent Chang and Ripley simultaneously. And indeed because Parker like every other attorney is an "officer of the court," he is as beholden to the judicial system as he is to his client. He is in the service of both. A strict application of the Matthew rule would thus preclude anyone from ever serving as anybody else's attorney.

A more promising approach would be for Parker to foresee at once that conflicting obligations are a possibility and to withdraw from the case. When Flynn, Ripley, and Chang sit down to tell their problem to Parker (who has not yet agreed to be their attorney), Parker must anticipate that, given the occurrence of certain events, he will be faced with an actual conflict of obligation if he agrees to represent all three clients. The bus company may file a countersuit against Flynn and the jury may find Flynn liable for the injuries sustained by the two passengers. If these things happen—and there is no way effectively to prevent their occurrence—Parker will be required to betray at least one of his clients. For that reason he may agree to represent Flynn or he may agree to represent Chang and Ripley; he may not agree to represent all three. The bare possibility that a conflict of obligation may arise would require the conscientious attorney, under this rule, to decline simultaneous representation of potentially conflicting interests. A responsible attorney must therefore be sensitive to the potential for conflict and be ready to step aside should a conflict of obligation be a possibility. On this account, the Matthew rule should be modified to prohibit an attorney from agreeing to serve more than one client when there is any reason to believe that meeting professional obligations to one of the clients might make it impossible to meet professional obligations to the other.

Like the original Matthew rule, this version will effectively prevent the occurrence of actual conflicts of obligation. But also like the Matthew rule, it may be a more draconian measure than is justified by the problem it seeks to prevent. For one thing, it will mean that the general public will have to support many more attorneys. Unless cases are dropped, additional lawyers will have to be employed whenever a potential conflict of obligation arises. While this may be financially beneficial for those in the legal profession, it may cause an erosion of public trust in lawyers, especially if less drastic measures can do the job.[2]

The presence of multiple attorneys may also promote more litigiousness than is necessary. Where Chang and Ripley might be able to reach agreement with Flynn in an informal setting, it may be that such agreement will be difficult if both sides are represented by attorneys *before* an actual conflict has arisen. Geoffrey C. Hazard has helpfully illuminated this point.

> In respect to these broader terms in which conflict of interest is defined, the culture of law itself is a contributing determinant. The point can be made more clearly by considering cultures that sharply contrast in this regard. In this country, the ideals of due process, private property, and formal equality

[2] See Thomas D. Morgan, "The Evolving Concept of Professional Responsibility," 90 *Harvard Law Review* (1977): 702, 727.

(that is, equality in legal status) lead to the definition of human relationships in legal terms. They also imply that adjudication is a normal and in some sense an ideal form of resolving disputed relationships. A derivative of this premise is that the role of partisan advocate and counselor is a normal, primary, and perhaps idealized one for a lawyer to play. By way of sharp contrast, in Japanese culture the ideals of concord and deference to traditional authority predominate. The definition of human relationships in legal terms is regarded as the exhibition of something like anti-social tendencies. A derivative of this premise is that in Japan it is uncommon to resort to legal assistance and more uncommon still for lawyers to assume the role of partisan rather than neutral expositor of the law. Within both countries, certainly this one, the degree of "legalism" in definition of relationships varies with specific context, as already suggested. But when an American lawyer is consulted, the client's orientation to the problem is usually adversarial, precisely because the lawyer's normal or expected role is that of partisan. Hence the fact that a client has consulted a lawyer can signify that the client contemplates a legally assertive course of action and itself is a step in the direction of defining a divergency of interest as a conflict of interest.[3]

If the potential for conflict of interest is well enough understood by the attorney and the prospective clients, it may be that agreement can be reached as to what the attorney's obligations will be should events occur that might precipitate an actual conflict of obligations. The obligations that Parker has to clients, he has because they have delegated responsibilities to him. If the clients explicitly forbear delegating to Parker responsibilities that may give rise to a conflict of obligations, then, since Parker cannot then find himself in an actual conflict, he will have no reason to decline representation of all three. Let us see how this might work.

The scene is once again Parker's initial interview with Flynn, Chang, and Ripley. The subject of the conversation is whether Parker will agree to represent any or all of the three in their proposed lawsuit against the bus company. The three potential clients have just completed recounting to Parker their story of the mishap and its consequences. Parker speaks:

"Based on what you all tell me, the three of you appear to have a solid case against the bus company. You are all in agreement that the accident was caused by the bus driver. If the rest of the evidence holds up, we would have a very good chance of prevailing at trial. But the bus company will not take this lying down. We can expect that they will file a countersuit against you, Ms. Flynn, and try to prove that the accident was your fault. From what you all tell me, it doesn't look as though they will succeed. But they might. No one can be certain which way the jury will go. If the jury finds you to be at fault, you will be held liable for the injuries your two friends have sustained. That will be a problem for you, and it may be a problem for your two friends. But it will also be a problem for me.

"As Ms. Flynn's attorney, I would ordinarily have the responsibility of advising

---

[3] From Geoffrey C. Hazard, Jr., *Ethics in the Practice of Law* (New Haven, Conn.: Yale University Press, 1978). Copyright by Seven Springs Farm Center. Reprinted by permission of the author and publisher.

her on whether she should file an appeal in the hope of getting a new trial and over-turning the jury's judgment against her. The bus company will have won its lawsuit against you, Ms. Flynn, but there may be something we can do about it on appeal. If there is, while that will be a good thing for you, it may not be such a good thing for your two friends here. An appeal and a new trial will take a great deal of time, and during that period, Mr. Chang and Mr. Ripley, you will not have received any money to pay your medical bills. You will essentially have won your case, and yet, because of my responsibilities to Ms. Flynn, I will be doing work that will delay your payment and possibly subject you to the difficulties of an appeal. If we are 'successful' on appeal, there could be a second trial that would probably not net you one extra penny. Just as I would ordinarily have an obligation to advise and to represent Ms. Flynn in connection with her appeal, I would ordinarily have an obli-gation not to work to overturn any judgment in your favor. In short, I think that any responsible attorney would have some reservations about taking on all three of you as clients.

"There may be, however, something that we can do now that will prevent such a conflict from arising later on. For example, if you, Ms. Flynn, were to stipulate now in our agreement that I am to have no responsibility to advise you and no re-sponsibility to represent you concerning any matter that may arise subsequent to the jury's verdict in this case, then I believe that that would take care of my reserva-tions. I will advise you now that if the jury should return a judgment against you, it would be wise immediately to seek legal counsel on the question of appeal. I will be happy to suggest the names of several attorneys who would be able to help you to make your decision, should the need arise. On the other hand, if you two gentle-men were to stipulate now in our agreement that I am being retained, not merely to press the claims that you three have against the bus company, but equally to defend Ms. Flynn against any countersuit the company might file against her—at trial, on appeal, and if necessary at retrial—then it may be that we can reach agreement in that way. Perhaps we will want to discuss the responsibility for fees in the event it becomes necessary to file for an appeal. In any case, if we decide to go this second route, I would want to have it clearly stated in our agreement that the appeals pro-cess may delay and even jeopardize any payment to you that the courts may find owing.

"There is possibly a third option which the three of you may wish to consider. We could agree that in the event that the jury returns a judgment against Ms. Flynn, I will have neither the responsibility to advise her nor the authority to represent her on appeal and thereafter unless the two of you explicitly consent to my doing so in full understanding of what the consequences might be.

"I think that I can live quite comfortably with any of these three options. It will probably be less expensive and there will be less duplication of effort if the three of you proceed, for now, with one attorney. But you should consider carefully that your interests might diverge, now or later on, and that it may be better to bring in a second attorney or to accept that it may be costly to some of you if I work to meet all the responsibilities you have delegated to me. Why don't you talk over these arrangements among yourselves, and if one of them seems suitable, I will be happy to draw up the appropriate agreement. On the other hand, if you feel it is better to go with separate attorneys, I will be happy to recommend several who can do the work."

Here, attorney Parker is treating a potential conflict of obligation, not as a flashing red signal to stop, but rather as a problem that can be resolved to the advantage of his clients. When a potential conflict of obligation becomes apparent, it is clear that the first step ought to be disclosure. The lawyer-client relationship tends to be an unfamiliar one to many lay persons, and explaining the problem can serve to clarify the nature of an attorney's obligation to a client. The second step, on this analysis, would be to set out ways in which the dilemma can be prevented from arising. Is it possible for clients to specify and limit the attorney's responsibility and authority so that the conflict cannot arise? Can clients explicitly waive certain rights or disavow expectations in order to consent to multiparty representation that would otherwise be ethically questionable? Is it possible adequately to advise clients in advance of those circumstances under which independent counsel should be sought? At the very minimum—and this may not be enough—the attorney should tell clients precisely what he or she will do in the event that a conflict of obligations arises and should secure from each client a consent that is informed by adequate knowledge of the consequences. What is suggested here is not so much a rule as a set of ethical strategies. To be sure, there will be many occasions in which a conscientious attorney, committed to doing the best for clients, can do nothing better than decline simultaneous representation. But it is often possible for an ethically competent lawyer to fashion a framework for cooperation that will serve all of the clients well.[4]

Our discussion of conflict of obligation has focused thus far on problems arising in simultaneous representation of divergent interests. But similar problems arise out of successive representations. Although most of an attorney's obligations to a client end when the lawyer-client relationship is dissolved, there is one that does not: The obligation of confidentiality typically comes into play in conflicts involving the former client.

For several years Mr. Gould refers legal questions arising in the course of his business to Kimura, his attorney. As Gould's business grows, he eventually takes his legal matters to another firm. Several years afterwards, Mrs. Gould shows up in Kimura's office to talk with him about getting a divorce from her husband. Because of Kimura's earlier relationship with Mr. Gould, Kimura knows a fair amount about the businessman's assets. He may have information that could be very useful to Mrs. Gould if there is litigation regarding a property settlement. But at the same time, Kimura is under an obligation not to disclose the information to anyone un-

---

[4] One option that Parker does not discuss is that Chang and Ripley sue the bus company *and Flynn* for their injuries. Has a conflict of obligations prevented Parker from giving his best advice to two of his clients? Nor does Parker discuss with Flynn the possibility that Chang and Ripley may have caused the accident—and their own injuries—by interfering with Flynn's driving. Perhaps Ripley interfered, but not Chang.

less Mr. Gould's permission is obtained. If Kimura agrees to serve as Mrs. Gould's attorney in the divorce proceedings against the former client, he will have the obligation to serve as her "zealous advocate," using all the means at his disposal to prevail in the courts. If there is something Kimura has learned from his former client that is crucial or even helpful to his current client, Kimura will be caught in a second type of conflict of obligation. He must advise and represent his current client to the best of his ability; yet, at the same time, he may have information essential to her welfare that he is not at liberty to utilize or divulge. Once the actual conflict of obligations becomes apparent to Kimura, it becomes patently clear that he must withdraw immediately as Mrs. Gould's attorney. He must abandon her. Indeed, he is not even permitted to explain in any detail the reasons for his withdrawal; to do so may be to violate the confidences he is obligated to preserve.

Conflicts of obligations arising out of successive representation are not manageable in the same way as those arising out of simultaneous representation. There is no longer a continuing relationship with one of the parties and not always an opportunity to hammer out agreements to the advantage of all. It is also frequently a nice question whether, without first exploring in detail the nuances of a new client's case, there is a potential conflict of obligation arising out of confidential communications from a prior client. Suppose Kimura had handled only one or two minor matters twelve years ago. Suppose most of what Kimura learned while serving as Mr. Gould's attorney has since become generally known. Since it may be difficult if not impossible to determine in advance whether one has confidential information from a prior client that could be helpful or even critical to a potential client whom one is interviewing for the first time, attorneys should probably err on the side of caution and decline representation when there is a possibility that zealous advocacy may be incompatible with the preservation of a former client's confidences.

One possible solution is to obtain the former client's consent. Waiving confidentiality, Mr. Gould can explicitly permit Kimura to represent his wife in the divorce action. A second solution might be to put the new client on notice that the attorney might withdraw at any moment without explanation. Perhaps there are some clients who would accept representation under such conditions. But the attorney may have an obligation to the court not to abandon clients in the midst of litigation. More to the point, the sudden decision to abandon a client can itself compromise the former client's confidences. Mr. Gould's wife could infer that the attorney knows something that would be useful to her that he cannot tell her. For this reason, unless there is consent from the former client, an attorney should disqualify himself or herself from representing any client where the matters under consideration are substantially related to matters considered in representing a former client.[5] Good judgment is called for in making this decision.

An attorney's good judgment is also a requirement where vicarious disqualifica-

---

[5] This is essentially the standard applied in *T.C. Theater Corp.* v. *Warner Bros. Pictures,* 113 F. Supp. 265 (S.D.N.Y. 1953), and specified in the Model Rules of Professional Conduct.

tion is a possibility. Suppose it had not been Kimura who represented Gould but Kimura's law partner. Must Kimura then decline representation of Mrs. Gould? Or suppose it had been Mr. Kimura's wife who represented Mr. Gould in his business transactions, or merely the attorney with whom Kimura shared office space. Kimura may be comfortable in the knowledge that he knows nothing whatever about Mr. Gould's financial status, past or present. From Kimura's perspective, we no longer have a potential conflict of obligations. From Mr. Gould's perspective, however, we may have a towering appearance of impropriety. It may look for all the world as if Kimura is relying on confidential information gained from an earlier slender or indirect relationship with Gould, information that is now being used to further the cause of one who has it in for Gould. Moreover, Gould may not be able to elaborate on his suspicions and Kimura may not be able to defend himself against the charges without disseminating the very information that is intended to be confidential. In terms of its effect on clients' willingness to trust lawyers, the appearance of betrayal is every bit as damaging as the real thing. Clients may refrain from sharing their confidences with their attorneys because they fear that the information may someday be used against them. This will mean that attorneys may be less able to give clients good advice. Hence, conflict of obligation in successive client representations, as an ethical problem for the practitioner, merges gradually into the profession's obligation to prevent flagrant appearances of impropriety among its members.

It is in this context that we are brought to the final point in our discussion of conflicts of obligation. For if the evidence that a court is permitted to examine supports the conclusion that an attorney may have relied on confidential information entrusted to him (or to his partner) by his present adversary; if it appears that there was an opportunity for him to be entrusted with such information and that the information could have been utilized on behalf of his present client against the former client, then a court may well be inclined to disqualify him as the client's attorney and to vacate any judgment he may have gained on his client's behalf. As one court put it: "An attorney must avoid not only the fact, but even the appearance, of representing conflicting interests."[6] If the system of adjudication is to work, if it is to succeed in generating judicial decisions that are likely to be just and that the community can accept as just, it must preserve appearances. The trial may have been defective because one of the parties had improper or inadequate representation. Indeed, in *Jedwabney* v. *Philadelphia Transportation Co.* (on which we loosely based our saga of Parker, Flynn, Chang, and Ripley), the attorney, who we assume *was* horrified, stood by as the Company won a new trial because the driver of the automobile was not adequately informed of his attorney's potentially conflicting obligations. The judge felt that the driver had not been "given the chance to make an informed choice." In his dissenting opinion in the case, Justice Musmanno laments that the two injured passengers who had won their verdict must once again "be subjected to the turmoil, the expense, the loss of time, the worry and the agony

[6] *Edelman* v. *Levy*, 346 N.Y.S. 2d 347 (1973).

which accompany a trial—with the possibility of drowning in a river they have already crossed."[7] But the community has a competing interest in ensuring that judicial proceedings preserve the appearance of propriety. Clients may indeed be ill-served if attorneys neglect such conflicts. While this is not the whole reason for lawyer attention to the potential for conflict, it is certainly part of it.

CONFLICTS OF INTEREST:
PERSONAL AND STRUCTURAL

In the preceding section we have seen how attorneys can get into ethical trouble if their obligation to one client is in potential or actual conflict with their obligation to another. A second type of conflict occurs when attorneys themselves have interests that may incline them away from fulfillment of their obligations to clients. Problems of this general type can arise wherever there are clear obligations associated with a social position. Consider the following:

1. The Anodyne Pharmaceutical Corporation is introducing a new drug for the treatment of hypertension. In its effort to promote sales as the drug enters the market, it offers expensive premiums to physicians who prescribe sufficient quantities before a certain date. Physicians who do this can choose a home stereo system, an all-expenses-paid vacation for two in Hawaii, or a self-propelled lawnmower. Dr. Brisby switches his patients over to the new drug and opts for the Hawaiian vacation.

2. For the past nine years, the four to six hundred students who take Professor Darnay's introductory-level political science course each semester have been required to read *An Introduction to Politics* written by Professor Darnay himself. The book costs $30, and Professor Darnay collects $4 in royalties from the publisher for every copy that is sold. Professor Darnay is the only professor who teaches this course, and student advisors regularly recommend it for prelaw undergraduates. Because new editions of the text are published regularly and are specifically assigned by the instructor, used books are seldom available for purchase.

3. Wiggins is the purchasing agent for a small municipality. He has responsibility for the final decision on all significant purchases made by the city government. For the past seven years, the city has purchased all of its automobiles from Ray's Motors. Ray, the owner and general manager of the company, is Wiggins's brother-in-law.

Now let us examine some similar cases in legal settings.

---

[7] *Jedwabney* v. *Philadelphia Transportation Co.*: see note 1 above. It is a nice question, but one we will table, whether the Company ought to have had the standing to complain to the court and to win an appeal on the basis of the conflict of obligation on the part of the other side's attorney. The injured party—the driver of the car—never saw fit to protest that he had been unfairly treated. On the other hand, since the driver's attorney also represented the passengers, is it reasonable to expect that the court would hear of the driver's complaint through his attorney? How might a judge decide if a new trial is required because one of the parties was possibly not properly represented?

4. Big Jake, a reputed underworld leader, has a reputation for distributing extravagant gifts whenever things go well. After prevailing in a criminal case against him, Jake sends expensive presents to the prosecuting attorney on the other side, to the judge, and to all twelve of the jurors.

5. Mullens, who has been struck by an automobile and is recovering from injuries, contacts Taney, an attorney, about suing the driver of the car. Taney declines to take the case but recommends that Mullens see Hargitty, a specialist in personal injury cases. Mullens seems agreeable and remains in the office while Taney telephones Hargitty and schedules an initial interview. Taney and Hargitty have a standing agreement that whenever Taney refers a case to her, Hargitty will give him a small amount of work in connection with the case and will pay him one-third of whatever fee she obtains. Mullens is not aware of the arrangement.

6. Three years ago, in doing some estate planning, Scribner drafted a will for Whipple, who was then seventy-eight years old. Now Whipple has died, and his Last Will and Testament is in probate. The will that Scribner earlier prepared for his client provides that one-third of the deceased's substantial estate go to his "good friend and faithful attorney, Scribner."

To begin, let us note that in the first three of the foregoing situations, we are not looking at conflicting obligations. Each actor can be said to have a personal interest in the outcome of the transaction but not an obligation to pursue that interest. Dr. Brisby clearly has no obligation to accept the Hawaiian vacation. While Professor Darnay, one assumes, is not completely disinterested as regards the $4,000 he collects annually from students he requires to purchase his book, he has no obligation to collect these funds. Wiggins, one supposes, is not displeased that some of the city's business has gone to a member of his family; still, it would not have been wrong for him to step aside and allow someone else to select the most competitive bid and issue the contract. There is certainly no obligation to take every opportunity to enrich oneself (and one's relatives), especially when one occupies a social position in virtue of which one is beholden to others, as the doctor is to his patients, as the teacher is to his students, and as the purchasing agent is to the citizens of his community.

Nor are we necessarily looking at a series of betrayals. Dr. Brisby's patients, let us suppose, will not suffer for having been switched to the new medication. Other conscientious professors use Darnay's *An Introduction to Politics.* And Wiggins's municipality is not being made to pay exorbitant prices for second-rate automobiles. We will suppose then that Dr. Brisby's patients, Professor Darnay's students, and the citizens of Wiggins's municipality are not the victims of deliberate efforts to shortchange them; indeed, they are not victims at all. Under different circumstances, other doctors, professors, or purchasing agents might reasonably have made the same choices without the extra incentives.

Let us suppose then that, despite their expectation that they might receive expensive gifts from the overjoyed Jake, the prosecutor, the judge, and the jurors do their very best not to let possible benefits for themselves affect either their effort or their judgment; even without Jake's reputation for largesse, the outcome might have been the same. Let us suppose that Taney has the highest regard for Hargitty's legal abilities and might well choose to go to her himself if the need arose. Finally, let us accept that Scribner did not twist Whipple's arm in order to get him to sign the will; it was Whipple's own idea to give a portion of the estate to Scribner, and, while Scribner did not object, other attorneys might well have found the bequest to Scribner to be unexceptional had they been drafting the will. Our concern here is not with the reasonableness or unreasonableness of the actions undertaken in behalf of the clients; it is rather with the acceptances of the gift and the referral fee and with the drafting of the will, enriching fiduciaries who are beholden to others.

It might be plausibly suggested that what is ethically perilous in these cases is the possibility that judgment might be affected despite the care taken to avoid influence. Subconsciously, the expectation that one has something to gain may play a role in one's deliberations. To the extent that this is so (*ex hypothesi*; one cannot know it is not so), one may not be doing the most responsible work that can be done under the circumstances. While we might suppose in setting up our examples that other attorneys, judges, etc., might have acted similarly even without a comparable personal interest in the outcome, it may not be possible for one who is subject to a conflicting personal interest to be equally confident about what a disinterested judgment would look like. Without the attorney's knowing about it, a personal interest in the matter may compromise the ability to exercise independent professional judgment on behalf of a client. Standing to benefit from specific advice or representation, the attorney also has an interest in underestimating the degree to which advantage to self may interfere with the fulfillment of obligations to the client. And so for many—perhaps for all—it may be ethically imprudent to trust one's own opinion that professional judgment will be unaffected by personal interest.

Still, an attorney might be confident—let us suppose, for the sake of discussion, reasonably so—that her independent judgment will not be compromised by a personal interest. Is there reason still for the responsible attorney to be concerned about conflict of interest? Does "reasonable" confidence that independent judgment will not be affected suffice to satisfy an attorney's doubts about the propriety of proceeding in the face of a conflicting personal interest?

In a professionalized legal system such as ours, people are not expected to understand their legal situation without professional counsel, nor are they expected to be able to secure that to which they are legally entitled unless they have access to professional services available only through licensed attorneys. Clients are thus sitting ducks for unscrupulous attorneys, and in general they know it. Legal advice may further the attorney's interests more than the client's, and legal action can benefit the attorney at the client's expense. For this reason loyalty to the client must be an overriding obligation of attorneys if the general public is to trust members of the legal profession. To the extent that lay persons believe that people generally pursue their own interests, attorneys must make a special effort to try to get across to clients that it will be the clients' interests that will be determinative of the lawyer's advice and representation and that the lawyer's personal interests will not compromise that loyalty to the clients. It is clearly part of the profession's responsibility that this be done. It is also in the profession's enlightened interest.

The duty of loyalty thus has two parts. There is a guarantee that the profession makes to a client on behalf of the attorney that he or she will exercise independent judgment on the client's behalf and will be a zealous advocate in representing the client's interests within the judicial system. That part is satisfied when the attorney is confident that significant personal interests will not interfere with independent judgment or zeal. But, additionally, there is a second guarantee: that the attorney will not give reason to believe that the loyalty has been compromised. A lawyer may be confident that potentially compromising influences are not having an effect, and we may suppose that such confidence is reasonable in the light of the attorney's experience. But one cannot be equally confident that others, believing attorneys to be as self-interested as anyone else, will be ready to accept the attorneys own assurances that personal interests played no role in professional judgment. In each of the six cases above, the existence of the conflicting personal interest calls into question the propriety of an action that would otherwise be unexceptional. If it becomes known that physicians participate in Anodyne's sales promotion plan, patients may be less willing to accept the advice of doctors. One cannot be sure whether a prescription is being written because the patient needs a new medication or because the physician needs a self-propelled lawnmower. Likewise, the students in Professor Darnay's class may underestimate the significance of his book on the grounds that it is being assigned, not because of some independent judgment as to its quality and appropriateness, but rather because Darnay needs the supplement to his income. His action may be construed as exploitative of his students. Thirdly, Wiggins's award of the contract to his brother-in-law can call into doubt the integrity of the governmental process. Suspicions will be aroused and confirmed that govenrment offices do not serve the community so much as they serve the officeholders.

It is not difficult to appreciate how the fairness of Big Jake's trial is called into question by his distribution of expensive gifts. By way of comparison, suppose that the losing quarterback in an important professional football game were to receive from the owner of the winning team the sum of $100,000 in a brown paper bag. Suppose it were widely publicized that this transfer had taken place only a few hours after the conclusion of the game, a game in which the quarterback, normally a star player, had played badly. Consider how the bare fact that the money had changed hands can compromise the integrity of the game. Apart from whether or not the quarterback deliberately shaved points or threw the game; apart from whether or not the payments were made in satisfaction of some agreement made earlier; in the light of the payment, we have good reason to wonder whether what took place in the stadium was a genuine football game or an elaborate charade engineered to create the appearance of a fair test. Under the circumstances, the outcome of the game gives us scant reason to believe that the winners were the better football players. Likewise, if a trial is to serve as a social procedure for settling disputed questions, it is crucial that key participants in the transaction keep themselves above reproach. As with the role of quarterback, the positions of judge, prosecutor, and juror can create golden opportunities for self-enrichment at the expense of the apparent integrity of the process. The social positions themselves would lack point in the absence of a commitment not to benefit oneself in ways that *can be construed* as abusive of the privileges attaching to the roles. Thus, with only a few minor exceptions, the American Bar Association Code of Judicial Conduct (adopted in 1972) provides that "[n]either a judge nor a member of his family residing in his household should accept a gift, bequest, favor, or loan from anyone. . . ." Specifically barred is the acceptance of gifts from donors whose interests have come or are likely to come before the judge. Comparable constraints are applicable to the roles of juror and prosecutor.

Taney's referral of the Mullens case to Hargitty raises questions that are similar to those in the Dr. Brisby example. The existence of the referral fee calls into question the purpose of Taney's advice: Is it being given for the client's benefit or for the attorney's? Even if the attorney's recommendation is sound and the client is not being charged an unreasonable amount, few lay people, unschooled in the intricacy of the legal process, are likely to believe Taney when he says, with a straight face, that the kickback had no influence whatever on his professional judgment. To the extent that such referral fees are customary, the profession runs the risk that the general public will become aware of the practice and will look upon such recommendations with cynicism.[8]

Scribner's decision to draft the Whipple will, making himself a beneficiary, raises a different problem. Since Scribner *was* carrying out Whipple's instructions (and since Whipple is now dead), there is no occasion here for a client to lose trust. If eyebrows are raised at all, they will be those of the disinherited friends and relatives. Instead of decisively settling Whipple's intentions regarding the disposition of his estate, Scribner's document raises questions of undue influence and overreaching on the attorney's part, perhaps even questions of fraud arising out of the fiduciary relationship. Roman law would not permit the individual drawing a will to receive a legacy under it, and today the laws of some states provide that such a circumstance give rise either to a presumption or an inference of undue influence.[9] Not only is it the case that Scribner may not receive the portion of the estate that Whipple wanted him to have; his interest as a beneficiary of the will he was drafting can suffice to void the entire document. Since he is a beneficiary, Scribner's own testimony regarding the validity of the will can be called into question. Clearly, if Scribner had wanted to do his best work for his client, he would have suggested, without recommending names, that Whipple retain some other attorney of his own

---

[8] Though there are differences in the way they approach the problem, the Canons of Professional Ethics (Canon 34, Division of Fees), the Code of Professional Responsibility (DR 2-107, Division of Fees Among Lawyers), and the Model Rules of Professional Conduct (Rule 1.5, Fees) each prohibit the financial arrangement contemplated by Taney and Hargitty. Nothing, however, would prohibit Taney from charging Mullens a reasonable fee for advising him to retain Hargitty.

[9] *State* v. *Horan,* 21 Wis. 2d 66, 123 N.W.2d 488 (1963).

choosing to draft a codicil providing for the bequest.[10] In part, this is a matter of prudence and competence. To do any less is to do less than one's best work for one's client. But in this case the expected outcome of the shoddy legal workmanship involves a substantial benefit for the attorney. The conflict of interest could hardly be more glaring.

The conflicts of interest that are of most concern to the legal profession are those in which the attorney reaps a substantial financial benefit quite apart from payment for work done on the case. But as all of us value things other than money, the possibilities for conflicts of interest are perhaps as far-ranging as human desire itself. Service to a client can suffer if an attorney is uncomfortable unless in control of the client or, alternatively, uncomfortable unless the client is involved in the making of all decisions; if the attorney is worried about being too aggressive or not aggressive enough; or if the attorney is insufficiently concerned or too much concerned about competency to handle a client's problem. Conflicts can arise as a consequence of assuming too many responsibilities. Which client's affairs can be put on a back burner? Which pressing problem am I going to neglect today?[11] Becoming a responsible attorney is in large measure a matter of coming to understand the personal tensions here and learning to manage or to avoid the problems. It is often difficult to adapt one's self to the constraints of a professional role.

Some conflicts of interest, however, are neither personal in the sense just discussed nor the product of some special financial interest. These cannot be averted merely by referring the case to another attorney. Such conflicts are systemic: rooted in the institutional context of the professional role. Attorneys are paid for their work, and, under the hourly fee arrangements governing much attorney income, there is an ineradicable conflict of interest every time a lawyer advises a client to get legal help with a problem and that he or she is available to do the job. The conflict comes to the fore also whenever a professional advises a client to purchase additional professional services. The lawyer has a clear financial interest in the advice. Some may think the problem could be ameliorated if attorneys were paid flat salaries in prepaid legal-services plans rather than on an hourly rate or a fee-for-service basis. But, instead of solving the problem, this arrangement merely changes its effect. The employee on a flat salary can be supposed to have an interest in working less for the same amount of money. Thus the incentive for a salaried attorney might be to say to prospective clients, not that they need professional services when they do not, but rather that they do not need professional services when in fact they do.

The problem is well understood in the medical context. The fee-for-service system has for years been criticized for encouraging unnecessary medical treatment. Conversely, health maintenance organizations (HMOs) which pay doctors on a sal-

---

[10] This is the advice given by Henry Drinker, *Legal Ethics* (New York: Columbia University Press, 1953), p. 94.

[11] A useful source here is Andrew S. Watson, "A Psychological Taxonomy of Lawyer Conflicts," in his *The Lawyer in the Interviewing and Counselling Process* (Indianapolis: The Bobbs-Merrill Company, Inc., 1976), pp. 94–100.

ary basis have been criticized for not providing patients with needed medical services. The patient belonging to an HMO may spend less time in the hospital than a similar patient whose medical bills are paid for on a fee-for-service basis. But it is difficult to tell in practice whether the HMO patient is being deprived of needed care or whether the fee-for-service patient is paying for unneeded care. Conflicts of interest at this level require very careful specification of the concept of a need, medical or legal, and consideration of alternative incentive systems that can suffice to provide for those needs. The trick is to specify the details of a social structure that will assure the clients (or patients) that the services they receive are services they need, and the services they are denied are services they don't need. This is perhaps the most difficult question arising in the area of conflict of interest. At this writing, there is no favored answer.

CONFLICTS
AND THE CORPORATE CLIENT

Some of the most perplexing difficulties in legal ethics involve conflicts in the corporate setting. Often these are variatons on the plight of attorney Parker, considered earlier in this chapter. It will be recollected that Parker's "client" consisted of three people with potentially divergent interests. Likewise, the corporation is a "complex client." But unlike Chang, Ripley, and Flynn, a modern corporation has a legal, constitutional structure. In essence, the corporation is granted a legal recognition which has the effect of permitting its various agents to act in its name in the pursuit of lawful purposes. In addition to its agents, there are stockholders who nominally "own" the corporation and who are entitled to share in its profits.[12] Some may have purchased shares of stock hoping for a prompt increase in the price, while others may be looking for steady dividends in the long run. The owners may therefore have interests that are in conflict. In addition to the stockholders, there will be others with various legally secured rights to the corporation's assets: for example, creditors (employees, suppliers, banks) and plaintiffs who have been awarded judgments against the corporation. There is a board of directors, which is elected by the stockholders and which has formal responsibility for the corporation's policies. The board may be divided, with majority and minority members. And there is management, which has responsibility for the day-to-day operation of the corporation. Heading management is the chief executive officer (CEO or president), who is appointed by the board of directors. Until recently most corporate law was practiced within law firms, private organizations (usually partnerships) with multiple clients. In a partnership, each partner can be held liable for the wrongful conduct of each

---

[12] On corporations as property, see Lawrence Becker, "Private Property and the Corporation," in W. Michael Hoffman, ed., *Proceedings of the Second National Conference on Business Ethics* (Washington, D.C.: University Press of America, 1979), pp. 257–67. On a range of broader issues regarding property, see Lawrence Becker and Kenneth Kipnis, eds., *Property: Cases, Concepts, Critiques* (Englewood Cliffs: Prentice-Hall, Inc., 1984).

one of the others. But in recent years the "in-house" corporate counsel has appeared. These attorneys are salaried employees of the corporation. The sole client is then, in a sense, the attorney's work environment.

Let us suppose that Baroni, senior partner of Baroni and Sells, receives an urgent call to meet with Mishkin, the CEO of Anodyne Pharmaceutical Corporation, B & S's biggest client. Mishkin and Baroni have worked together for twelve years on various corporate problems; in fact, it was Mishkin who initially retained B & S on behalf of Anodyne. The men are friends. Mishkin takes a chair in Baroni's office and clears his throat.

"It may be," he says, "that I have been involved in authorizing 'questionable payments' to foreign government officials in order to boost company sales. Of course there are no records of these expenditures on our books: All payments were laundered through multiple intermediaries."

While Mishkin is speaking, Baroni is rapidly drawing conclusions. The Foreign Corrupt Practices Act makes it a crime for an American corporation to pay foreign government officials in order to obtain business. The corporation can be heavily fined and its officers jailed. Additionally, the Securities and Exchange Commission requires publicly owned companies such as Anodyne periodically to issue accurate and complete financial statements as a condition for their stock to be bought and sold in the market. It is a requirement that questionable foreign payments be disclosed. What Mishkin is saying may mean that there is inaccuracy or incompleteness in some of the financial statements that Anodyne has filed with the SEC. Baroni senses that things may become messy for Mishkin and Anodyne.

But now a second more fundamental problem emerges. Baroni is *not* Mishkin's lawyer. Rather, Baroni's firm is in the service of Anodyne as its retained attorney. While Mishkin speaks, it begins to dawn on Baroni that it is his job to further the interests of Anodyne, and that what is good for Anodyne could conceivably be very bad for Mishkin.

But how is Baroni supposed to know what is good for Anodyne? There is no problem if, as far as Baroni is concerned, Anodyne *is* Mishkin. What is good for Anodyne is what Mishkin says is good for Anodyne. If Mishkin says that the best thing for Anodyne to do is to keep its board of directors in the dark about the problem, who is Baroni to disagree? Mishkin is president of Anodyne, the chief executive officer, overseeing all of the operations of the company. The board of directors, in hiring Mishkin, has delegated to him the responsibility for day-to-day management of the corporation. Mishkin can hire or fire Anodyne's lawyer. The man's opinion surely must be given weight.

But now Baroni considers that there must be some limits to Mishkin's authority to pursue what he says are the legitimate and proper purposes of Anodyne Pharmaceutical. If Mishkin had been channeling Anodyne's funds into his private accounts, or if he had been ordering the assassinations of the competition's key personnel, surely then it would be clear that the boundaries of legitimacy and propriety had been overstepped. If there are discernible limits to the authority of a chief executive officer—limits to the authority granted to him by the board of directors that

hired him—and if an attorney has good reason to believe that a CEO is going beyond those limits, isn't the attorney for the corporation then accountable to the
board rather than to the CEO? Since Anodyne's board of directors doesn't have the
authority to permit Mishkin to act in violation of the law, Mishkin has clearly exceeded any authority the board has to give *if* he has broken the law. Moreover, it
may turn out that the best course for Anodyne is to cooperate in the criminal conviction of their chief executive officer. Since that course is pretty clearly not best
for Mishkin, it can be supposed that in his presidency of Anodyne he has an obvious conflict of interest. In acting as CEO, will Mishkin be wanting to protect the
interests of the corporation or his own? Perhaps, just for a moment, Baroni should
consider that his primary obligation may be to the board of directors, which "personates" his client.

If, for the purposes of this matter, the board of directors is the client, then perhaps the attorney's duty is to apprise the board—*if* that is what the board would
want the attorney to do. On the assumption that the board consists of honorable
men and women who would want to know about it if management had conducted
unauthorized, illegal, and possibly economically imprudent activities, Baroni should
convey the substance of his conversation to the board as soon as possible. There
may be a pressing need to map a corporate strategy that is suited to the exigencies
of the moment. Part of a corporate lawyer's job is to be a fire fighter, to prevent
manageable blazes from erupting into conflagrations. Baroni's well-trained legal
nose smells smoke.

But isn't Mishkin owed a duty of confidentiality? Didn't he call for Baroni's help
when he needed legal advice? Hasn't Baroni worked for years to develop a relationship of trust and confidence with Mishkin, continually stressing the importance of
openness to the corporation's counsel? But while Mishkin did call Baroni for help,
Baroni did not answer the call as Mishkin's lawyer. Of all people, Mishkin should
know that Baroni is the attorney for Anodyne Pharmaceutical: Mishkin himself
hired Baroni for the job.

It begins to dawn on Baroni that the chief executive officer thinks he is talking
to *his*—the CEO's—attorney. But if Anodyne, personated in its board of directors,
is the real client, and if there is a strong possibility that Anodyne and Mishkin have
interests that are in conflict (that is, the satisfaction of the interests of one precludes the satisfaction of the interests of the other), then, though Mishkin thinks he
is talking to his own lawyer, it may be that in fact he is talking to his adversary's
lawyer. It may be that everything he is saying to Baroni, his trusted friend, will be
used by Anodyne to put him in jail.

Betrayal is only possible within a relationship of trust and confidence. It can occur when, on invitation, we make ourselves vulnerable to others in the hope that we
will find counsel, compassion, and understanding and, instead, discover that our
openness has become an avenue of attack. Betrayal breeds cynicism. Alan Dershowitz in his *The Best Defense*[13] recounts an interchange in an unnamed movie:

[13] Alan M. Dershowitz, *The Best Defense* (New York: Random House, Inc., 1982), p. 358.

First lawyer:	Don't you trust me?
Second lawyer:	Absolutely.
First lawyer:	Me neither.

But surely, even if Mishkin is not Baroni's lawyer, he is at least Baroni's friend. And while Baroni may not have an obligation of confidentiality as Mishkin's lawyer, surely he has an obligation of confidentiality as his friend. And friends do not betray one another. Mishkin may expect that Baroni will not betray a friend. But if Baroni chooses to protect Mishkin by concealing his disclosures from the board, he will have to trust Mishkin to conceal his own duplicity. For to the extent that Mishkin knows that Baroni understood what Mishkin said, Mishkin knows that Baroni will be concealing from the board information that perhaps it ought to have. What the two *friends* need is a charade. They need to be able to "agree" on a common story without agreeing on a common story. Baroni can say: "I am not certain I understood you. It may be that you are talking about some kind of personal problem that I don't think I can help you with. Good day." Following up on the hint, Mishkin can respond: "On second thought, it seems to me that Anodyne doesn't have a problem here. I am sorry I took your time." The two are now in agreement that Baroni never received the information from Mishkin. In their conspiracy against Anodyne, friendship is thus preserved and the corporate employer/client betrayed.

Baroni is in a classic conflict of obligation, much like the one that perplexed Dexter in the boxing ring with his son: He is going to have to choose between being a bad lawyer and being a bad friend. Perhaps, as Anodyne's lawyer, he was being unprofessional when he befriended Mishkin. On the other hand, it was important for him, as an attorney, to invite a relationship of trust and confidence with the chief executive officer. Mishkin can hardly be faulted for thinking of Baroni as more than simply Anodyne's attorney.

It seems very wrong for Baroni to sit there while Mishkin goes on talking to him. Mishkin has a terrible misapprehension about what is happening to him. Though he does not know it, he may be damaging himself horribly. Perhaps what Baroni ought to do is to warn Mishkin (out of friendship? out of fairness? out of decency?) as police do when, after an arrest, they give the suspect his "Miranda warning." "You have a right to an attorney. . . . Anything you say may be held against you." Baroni should read Mishkin his rights, admonishing him that anything the CEO says may have to be disclosed to the board of directors and possibly others as well. Perhaps Baroni should say something like this:

"As attorney for Anodyne, I must warn you that our conversations are not covered by the obligation of confidentiality. That obligation only protects my client, in this case Anodyne. Anything you tell me may have to be revealed to, at a minimum, the board of directors. If you go on, it may be wise to assume that in talking with me you are disclosing to the board."

But such a warning may not suffice. In the first place, the very words that create the occasion for such a warning also put Anodyne's attorney on notice that something may be seriously amiss with his client's legal affairs. If it is reasonable, on the basis of what has been said, to warn Mishkin—who is not the client—why is it not equally reasonable, on the same facts, to warn the client? Baroni cannot bring it about that the conversation did not occur, nor can he deliberately forget that the conversation took place. And, as Anodyne's attorney, it is not proper for him to "wall off" a potentially valuable part of his consciousness, to ignore something he has reason to believe is true, if he is to discharge his responsibility to protect his client's interests. In its discussion of conflict of interest, the Model Rules hold that loyalty to a client is impaired "when a lawyer cannot consider, recommend, or carry out an appropriate course of action for the client because of the lawyer's other responsibilities or interests. The conflict in effect forecloses alternatives that would otherwise be available to the client."[14] Perhaps, as Anodyne's loyal attorney, Baroni should sit there quietly, listening attentively and drawing Mishkin out whenever it is appropriate. When the CEO has finished incriminating himself, Baroni should bring the matter to the board at once. Unimpaired loyalty to the client would seem to require the betrayal of his friend.

But we have been assuming that the members of the board of directors would, if given the choice, elect to be informed of their CEO's impropriety. This may not be so. Often board members will prefer to rely wholly on management, routinely ratifying its decisions and passively reviewing reports and statements. Even though the chances are slim that the directors themselves will be subject to a legal judgment against them personally, they may prefer not to become involved in litigation. Christopher Stone has written:

> In bending over backwards to protect the directors, top-level management is inclined to shield them from "bad news" of potential corporate vulnerability. . . . This may seem odd to the layman, given . . . the low risk that the directors, even if sued, will ultimately suffer any out-of-pocket loss. But there is a special sort of conservatism that I have personally witnessed to operate in this setting. Everyone recognizes that the directors did not bargain even for the "hassle" of a lawsuit; no one wants to get them involved. What they don't know is often judged potentially less embarrassing than what they might discover.[15]

Suppose then that the board will require an ironclad case against Mishkin before it will entertain criticism of him. Suppose they can be expected to fire attorneys who are foolish enough to do end runs around management, reporting their mere suspicions directly to the board. If Baroni has good reason to believe that the members of the board don't want to get involved—reason to believe that they would rather see the corporation endure third-degree burns than be disturbed themselves by the sound of the fire alarm—then perhaps it is Mishkin who personates the corporation. In such cases it might seem that the board has essentially delegated to the

[14] Model Rules, Comment on Rule 1.7.

[15] In many cases this assumption is false. See Christopher Stone, *Where the Law Ends* (New York: Harper & Row, Publishers, Inc., 1975), p. 147.

chief executive officer not only the responsibility for management but the board's responsibilities as well. If Anodyne's board is like this, perhaps Baroni should simply roll up his sleeves and start protecting Mishkin's hide. It may be that Anodyne's interests can be served at the same time, provided they are not in conflict with Mishkin's. If the board complains later on, Baroni need only say that while Mishkin clearly shouldn't have been given the authority he had—authority that he abused in directing the corporation's affairs illegally and in his own interests—the board never acted to take that authority away from him. Though Baroni may end up assisting Mishkin in actions that turn out to be damaging to Anodyne, maybe he can defend himself later on by claiming that the blame belongs to the board for appointing Mishkin in the first place.

But the legal profession's view has long been that a lawyer who is employed or retained by an organization owes loyalty to the organization "as distinct from its directors, officers, employees, members, shareholders or other constituents."[16] The approach developed in the Model Rules—Rule 1.13(a)—applies to the situation in which the corporation's attorney "knows" that an officer is engaged in action that is either in violation of a legal obligation to the corporation or illegal in a way that could be imputed to the corporation, and that such action is likely to result in substantial injury to the organization. In such cases an attorney may be required to refer the matter to a higher authority in the organization or, if necessary, to take further remedial action that the lawyer reasonably believes to be in the best interests of the organization. There is a requirement as well—in Rule 1.13(d)—that the attorney "in dealing with an organization's . . . officers, . . . shall explain the identity of the client when the lawyer believes that such explanation is necessary to avoid misunderstandings on their part." If Baroni gives Mishkin his Miranda warning, Mishkin will then understand that it may be necessary to disclose the matter to the board. (Must Baroni tell Mishkin about the five-year jail sentence for officers who violate the Foreign Corrupt Practices Act?) If, in spite of the warning, Mishkin tells all to Baroni, there may be no problem. Perhaps the matter can be competently cleared up without involving the board or anyone else in the company. But if Mishkin balks, afraid of what the consequences might be if he confesses, the lawyer may find himself cut off from sources of information at the company.

At this point the Model Rules substitute an epistemological problem for an ethical one. The question is not whether to disclose. It is, rather, "What does the lawyer know?" As noted above, Baroni can be required to blow the whistle on Mishkin only if he *knows* that the officer has violated the law in acting for the corporation or has violated an obligation to the organization, and if he knows that what the officer has done is likely to result in a substantial injury to Anodyne. But what Mishkin said was, "It *may* be that I have been involved. . . ." Baroni doesn't know, on the basis of what Mishkin has told him, that there *has* been a violation. Moreover, the likelihood of substantial injury is impossible for Baroni to determine without hearing what Mishkin has to say. And Mishkin has nothing to say to Baroni. In the

---

[16] Model Rules, Rule 1.13. See also the Code of Professional Responsibility, EC 5-18.

absence of the required knowledge, the Model Rules do not seem to be of much help to an attorney caught between a suspiciously silent officer and a deliberately hard-of-hearing board of directors. How thick does the smoke have to get before we *know* there is a fire?

In fact, the real problem here is not an epistemological one at all. It is a structural one involving the constitution of the corporate client. What must be admitted at once is that, under the circumstances, it is impossible for Baroni to serve the interests of Anodyne. The officers of the organization appear to be abusing their authority and the directors appear to be neglecting their responsibilities. The president doesn't want to talk to Baroni, and the board doesn't want to listen to him. Baroni can pretend to be Anodyne's attorney—he may continue to be paid as such—but he is not helping the client to deal appropriately with its legal problems. Because of the way in which the organization is constituted, Anodyne's attorney is unable to speak with his client.

In the Comment to Rule 1.13, the Model Rules contain the following:

> Clear justification should exist for seeking review over the head of the officer or employee normally responsible for it. The stated policy of the organization may define circumstances and prescribe channels for such review, and a lawyer should encourage the formulation of such policy.

Like virtually all organizations, corporations are social systems that formulate goals, gather information, make decisions, and act. Though more is required for organizational soundness, part of what is necessary is that relevant information make contact with the organization's decision procedure.[17] Good channels of communication are vital if a modern corporation is to be able to respond to its challenges. The Model Rules reflect an appreciation of this in the passage quoted above. If the organization is to pursue its purposes effectively and avoid injury, sound legal advice must reach the appropriate level of decision-making. When the legal problem is potentially very serious, the appropriate level of decision-making is going to be very high. The problem with the approach of the Model Rules is that it requires the attorney to break down the door of a reticent board of directors only when there is *knowledge* of seriously damaging wrongdoing. It is just the policy a deliberately negligent board would want: a board that would tell its employees to wait until they see the flames and feel the heat before ringing the fire alarm—and make sure it is a serious fire! In setting the standard of intellectual responsibility very high— knowledge—and in requiring warnings that will shut off the sources of information needed to meet that standard, the Model Rules do little to guarantee that the interests of the organization will be served by their attorneys.

What the example of Anodyne Pharmaceutical Corporation shows is that at a certain level of institutionalized thickheadedness, it is not possible for an organiza-

---

[17] On organizations as rational actors, see Amitai Etzioni, *The Active Society* (New York: Harper & Row, Publishers, Inc., 1975). Others who have written helpfully on the problem include Peter A. French, "The Corporation as a Moral Person," *American Philosophical Quarterly* 16 (1979): 207–15; and Christopher Stone, *Where the Law Ends.*

tion to have an attorney. (Imagine serving as an attorney for a crowd.) A lawyer who works for and is paid by such an organization may be defrauding the client. If what the organization wants (to the extent that it can formulate such an objective) is a procedure that will ensure that legal advice make contact with the appropriate level of decision-making, perhaps attorneys can assist in crafting the required organizational arrangements. But in the absence of an acceptable corporate constitution, it would seem to be unethical for an attorney to represent himself or herself as corporate counsel.

In many cases it will not be enough for the profession merely to "encourage" the setting up of sound channels of corporate communication. One effective approach to the problems would be for the profession to set standards for contracts between attorneys and their corporate clients. Such contracts, mandated by the profession, would authorize and require the corporation's attorney to report to a specific member or members of the board (or to a member of their staff) any substantive *evidence* that an agent of the corporation is engaged in action that is either in violation of a legal obligation to the corporation or illegal in a way that could be imputed to the corporation, where such action could result in substantial injury to the organization. The special director or directors designated for that purpose would have to be "outside directors"—individuals who are not also employed officers of the corporation. Many corporate boards already have "audit committees" that could serve in this capacity. The board of directors would have to agree, as a condition for its receiving the services of an attorney, to review such reports as a regular part of its periodic meetings. Needless to say, the requirement that such terms be agreed to by corporations as a condition for the receipt of legal services would have to be set by the profession as a whole. Otherwise firms that did not require such agreements might have competitive advantages in the market against firms that did. In taking such a step, the profession would be asserting that it is unethical to take a position as a fire fighter if the employer doesn't provide a fire alarm.

The problems with Anodyne resemble those that arise in connection with incapacitated clients. The Model Rules specify that a lawyer may "seek the appointment of a guardian, or take other protective action with respect to a client, only when the lawyer reasonably believes that the client cannot adequately act in the client's own interests." A corporation can act only through its agents. If its agents are unable or unwilling to act in the interests of the corporation, while the individual attorney may be unable to do anything to protect the client, the legal profession, acting collectively, may be able to do quite a bit.

Of course, where the board of directors is dominated by board members who are also officers of the corporation ("inside" directors), or if members of the board are themselves the problem, pillaging the corporation's assets for their own benefit, these measures will not suffice. But there may be others like them that will.

Chapter 4

Confidentiality in Criminal Practice

In the summer of 1973 a young woman named Susan Petz disappeared while camping in upstate New York. Shortly afterwards, following an extensive manhunt nearby, a 38-year-old mechanic named Robert Garrow was arrested and charged with the murder of Philip Domblewski, a young man who had been fatally stabbed while camping at about the time of the young woman's disappearance. Since Garrow was indigent, the court appointed Frank Armani and Francis Belge to act as his defense attorneys. Though the police couldn't prove it, they suspected that Garrow had been involved in other killings and disappearances. Thus, when Susan Petz's father traveled from Illinois to New York to find out what he could about what had happened to his daughter, the police suggested that he talk with Garrow's attorneys, Armani and Belge. Susan Petz's father talked with Belge, but the attorney said nothing about the whereabouts of the missing woman.

In fact both attorneys knew where Susan Petz was, or, more accurately, where her body was. Robert Garrow had given his attorneys details of several crimes he had committed. After raping and killing Susan Petz, he had left her body in an abandoned mine shaft. With the aid of a map drawn by their client, Armani and Belge were able to locate the mine shaft and take pictures of the body of their client's victim.[1]

It is difficult to exaggerate the concern that communities can have to solve grisly crimes and to apprehend and punish dangerous criminals. And the interest that a parent can have in learning the fate of a missing son or daughter must be accorded great weight in ethical deliberations. Thus arguments from security, justice, and compassion can all support the conclusion that attorneys Armani and Belge should have disclosed what their client had told them—and what they knew to be true—about the location of the body. Indeed there was considerable public outrage after Garrow confessed and it became apparent that Armani and Belge had withheld the truth. Letters to the editor excoriated the lawyers and the legal profession. One person wrote: "[I]f this is the lawyer's Code of Ethics, to put parents through hell,

---

[1] Jeffrey Frank Chamberlain, "Legal Ethics: Confidentiality and the Case of Robert Garrow's Lawyers," 25 *Buffalo Law Review* (1975): 221–22. This article contains numerous references to documentation relevant to the Lake Pleasant case, some of which is cited here.

then it's about time it be changed."[2] The mother of Susan Petz was quoted as say-ing "Oh my God . . . oh my God . . . isn't that illegal? I can't imagine anyone living with such a thing; it must be illegal."[3]

NONDISCLOSURE: THE LEGALITIES

The suggestion that Armani and Belge be punished for a criminal offense merits first consideration, for in the Anglo-American legal system citizens have no general legal obligation to report to the authorities what they know about criminal con-duct. Indeed, what would it be like if everyone—every neighbor, friend, relative— were a deputized agent of the prosecutor, *legally obligated* to pass along evidence of wrongdoing? Such an arrangement would be reminiscent of the "secret police" as-sociated with tyrannical forms of government. If a public choice is made to let citi-zens use their own discretion in deciding when to contact the authorities, there may be some loss of efficiency in apprehending criminals, but there may well be a net gain in the quality of social life. The point here is that it is not unreasonable to opt for a legal system, such as ours, in which there is no general legal duty to notify the authorities of inculpating evidence. If Armani and Belge acted wrongfully, it wasn't because they violated some such law or even some general rule that clearly ought to be embodied in law.

Of course, failure to bring evidence to the attention of others must be distin-guished from the deliberate concealment of evidence. If Armani and Belge had buried the body in the cave, if they had hidden the cave's entrance with debris, it could indeed have been a criminal offense: technically, misprision of a felony. Much of the literature on confidentiality suffers from not carefully distinguishing between the failure to assist the authorities in apprehending wrongdoers and active complicity in the crime itself. And too many of the legal profession's critics slide too easily from the premise that someone has not reported a crime to the conclu-sion that he shares guilt for it: That I know of a crime that I do not report does not entail that I share responsibility for the wrongdoing. At the very least, critics who rely on such a principle of complicity owe their readers an argument for it. We will consider questions of complicity in the next chapter; here it is not an issue.

A related point has to do with *special* legal obligations to bring forward evidence inculpating others. While there is no general legal duty to do so, a court may specifi-cally require an individual to appear in court and testify under oath. The power to subpoena witnesses ensures that relevant evidence will be available to a jury when a case is finally brought to trial. Clearly there is a weighty public interest in the avail-ability of the best evidence. An officer of the court (typically a sheriff) serves a potential witness with a legal document (a subpoena) and, in so doing, creates a

[2] *Herald Journal* (Syracuse), July 2, 1974, at 3, col. 4.

[3] *Times Union* (Albany), June 20, 1974, at 7, col. 1. Though the local prosecutor filed charges against the attorneys, their conduct was not found to be unlawful.

special legal obligation to appear in court to answer questions about some matter of interest to the court. While a citizen may legally choose not to volunteer evidence, if that person is subpoenaed and is asked for it, it must be given.

But the court's power to demand that testimony be given is limited by, among other things, the *legal privilege of confidentiality.* Arising out of the common law but often embodied in statutes, this is an exception to the general liability to be called to testify. A priest for example cannot be subpoenaed and required to disclose what he has been told in the privacy of the confessional. Likewise, the court cannot demand that a wife or husband give testimony against a spouse. In his classic discussion of confidentiality in *Evidence,* Wigmore lists four conditions that must be satisfied if the privilege is to obtain:

> Looking back upon the principle of privilege, as an exception to the general liability of every person to give testimony upon all facts inquired of in a court of justice, and keeping in view that preponderance of extrinsic policy which alone can justify the recognition of any such exception . . . , four fundamental conditions are recognized as necessary to the establishment of a privilege against the disclosure of communications:
>
> (1) The communications must originate in a *confidence* that they will not be disclosed.
>
> (2) This element of *confidentiality must be essential* to the full and satisfactory maintenance of the relation between the parties.
>
> (3) The *relation* must be one which in the opinion of the community ought to be sedulously *fostered.*
>
> (4) The *injury* that would inure to the relation by the disclosure of the communications must be *greater than the benefit* thereby gained for the correct disposal of litigation.
>
> Only if these four conditions are present should a privilege be recognized.[4]

Lawyers, or more properly their clients, enjoy this testimonial privilege. Its dimensions have also received their classic formulation in Wigmore:

> (1) where legal advice of any kind is sought (2) from a professional legal advisor in his capacity as such, (3) the communications relating to that purpose, (4) made in confidence (5) by the client, (6) are at his instance permanently protected (7) from disclosure by himself or by the legal advisor, (8) except the protection be waived.[5]

On Wigmore's view, if clients fear that what they confide to their attorneys may have to be revealed to the court, they will be apprehensive about consultation, and the process of adjudication may be seriously damaged. In order to encourage clients to be open with their lawyers, in order to promote freedom of consultation with skilled legal advisors, the testimonial privilege is instituted so that this source of fear

---

[4] John Henry Wigmore, *Evidence in Trials at Common Law,* Vol. 8 (Boston: Little Brown and Company, 1961), Section 2285, p. 527.

[5] Wigmore, *Evidence,* Section 2292, p. 554.

will be removed. As it is put in *McCormick's Handbook on the Law of Evidence,* the justification of the privilege is founded upon

> the theory that claims and disputes which may lead to litigation can most justly and expeditiously be handled by practised experts, namely lawyers, and that such experts can act effectively only if they are fully advised of the facts by the parties whom they represent. Such full disclosure will be promoted if the client knows that what he tells his lawyer cannot, over his objection, be extorted in court from the lawyer's lips.[6]

Clients—the holders of the privilege—are guaranteed that their legal advisors will not be subpoenaed to testify as to what was said in conversations with them; lawyers will not be subject to any special legal obligation to disclose confidential information.

If, as seems reasonable, we assume that what Robert Garrow said to his attorneys was communicated in the course of legal counseling and that he had not waived his privilege, it follows that Armani and Belge were immune from being subpoenaed and subsequently compelled to disclose what they knew about their client's crimes. Not only were they not subject to any general legal obligation to disclose; they were immune from special legal obligations as well.

LEGALITY AND MORALITY

Though they are related, questions about the legality of disclosure—whether discretionary, legally prohibited, or legally obligatory—are separate from questions about the ethics of disclosure. The relationships between the questions are, however, at least two in number. In the first place, it may be that there is some ethical obligation to obey the law or, less strongly, that the legality of a contemplated action should be accorded weight in assessing whether or not it is ethical. If either of these is so, then the state of the law as expressed in statutes and judicial decisions may have a decisive bearing on the ethics of disclosure. But, as is well known, it is controversial whether there is a general ethical obligation to obey the law.[7] And, as the rich literature on the ethics of civil disobedience shows, even if there is such an obligation, it is equally controversial whether and, if so, when it is outweighed by other obligations. Of course, if attorneys have legal discretion to disclose or not to disclose, then the legality of an attorney's withholding or disclosure of information does not settle questions about its ethics. That a course of action is legal does not entail that it is ethical.

---

[6] Edward W. Cleary, *McCormick's Handbook on the Law of Evidence,* 2nd ed. (St. Paul: West Publishing Company, 1972), p. 175.

[7] See, for example, Robert Paul Wolfe, *In Defense of Anarchism* (New York: Harper & Row, Publishers, Inc., 1976); Alan Goldman, *The Philosophical Foundations of Professional Ethics* (Totowa: Rowman & Littlefield, 1980); Richard Wasserstrom, "The Obligation to Obey the Law," in Richard Wasserstrom, *Philosophy and Social Issues* (Notre Dame: University of Notre Dame Press, 1980), pp. 83–111; Robert Ladenson, "In Defense of a Hobbesian Conception of Law," *Philosophy and Public Affairs* 9 (1980): 134–59.

The second way in which the issues can be related is perhaps somewhat less controversial. If it is clear that attorneys are ethically required to withhold (or disclose) confidential communications, there is good reason to configure the law so that it does not prohibit attorneys from doing what they are ethically obligated to do. As Ronald Dworkin has shown in his widely read "On Not Prosecuting Civil Disobedience"[8] and in other works, legal reasons and ethical considerations are not so easily distinguished. Principles of "political morality" may well form an important part of our legal system. Accordingly, if there are sound ethical reasons why attorneys should or should not disclose, those reasons may carry legal weight as well.

But even if Dworkin be wrong, even if questions of ethics be wholly separate from questions of legality, a legal system imperils itself if it requires citizens to act unethically. As Judge Charles Wyzanski has put it:

> When the state through its laws seeks to override reasonable moral commitments, it makes a dangerously uncharacteristic choice. Law and morality are, in turn, debtors and creditors of each other. The law cannot be adequately enforced by the courts alone, or by courts supported merely by the police and the military. The true secret of legal might lies in the habits of conscientious men, disciplining themselves to obey the law they respect without the necessity of judicial and administrative orders. When the law treats a reasonable, conscientious act as a crime it subverts its own power. It invites civil disobedience. It impairs the very habits which nourish and preserve the law.[9]

Our assumption in what follows is that ethical considerations should be taken to be primary and that, as regards attorney-client confidentiality, sound law should not conflict with sound ethical judgment. Men and women who enter the legal profession should not be forced routinely to make tragic choices between acting unethically and acting illegally.

And so we are inexorably brought to the ethical issue. Notwithstanding what the law permits or requires, would it have been unethical for the attorneys to share what they knew with others? Was it unethical for them to keep it to themselves? It seems clear that the arguments for disclosure in circumstances like those which arose in the Lake Pleasant case can seem compelling. If likewise told of killings, other things being equal, few of us would believe it wrong to inform the authorities where Susan Petz's remains were to be found and who the killer was. Helping the law-enforcement authorities, the health officials, and the victim's relatives and friends is an important part of good citizenship. Because a failure to disclose seems clearly to stand in need of some special justification, there would appear to be a strong ethical presumption in favor of disclosure. Were the critics correct then in branding the attorneys' behavior as unconscionable?

---

[8] *New York Review of Books,* 10 (June 6, 1968): 14–21. Reprinted in Kenneth Kipnis, ed., *Philosophical Issues in Law: Cases and Materials* (Englewood Cliffs: Prentice-Hall, Inc., 1974), pp. 187–203, and as "Civil Disobedience," in Ronald Dworkin, *Taking Rights Seriously* (Cambridge: Harvard University Press, 1977), pp. 206–222.

[9] *United States* v. *Sisson,* 297 Fed. Supp. 902 (1969).

OATHS OF CONFIDENTIALITY

About a year after the trial, Frank Armani gave a reply to these questions in a speech to the Illinois Bar Association:

> I want to emphasize that my associate, Mr. Belge, and I took [the lawyer's oath] and that to us an oath is a very sacred thing. In retrospect however when we took this oath neither of us had the slightest idea of the awesome consequences it would someday carry. The taking of this oath and our attempt to live up to it has caused us and our families much anguish and pain.[10]

Armani's remarks suggest that the attorney's ethical obligation to withhold confidences is, at bottom, an instance of the familiar obligation to keep one's promises. If they took an oath never to disclose client confidences (or at least not to disclose them in this type of case), then, while the rest of us may have no excuse for not disclosing, the two attorneys do have such an excuse. As Sissela Bok has put it: "Once we promise someone secrecy, we no longer start from scratch in weighing the moral factors of a situation."[11] Thus whatever the ethical obligation of the attorneys to reveal what they knew about their client's crime, it had to be balanced against the conflicting obligation to honor a solemn oath.

The existence of such an oath can raise several issues. In the first place, there is the difficult question of how to balance against other obligations the special obligation of confidentiality that is created by a promise. Given that it is wrong to break one's promise and assuming that it is also wrong to withhold information that others need, what is the correct way of weighing these obligations against one another in ethical decision-making?

Answers may take either of two forms. In the first, one holds that there is a correct answer in each situation and that all one needs to do is to opt for it: Let the truth be known (or honor the promise) and that is the end of it. The decision-maker walks away with a clean conscience. The second type of answer involves an acknowledgment that there may be an element of tragedy in moral life. Regardless of one's ultimate choice, there are occasions when important ethical principles must be compromised and guilt known. As with Dexter, refereeing his son's boxing match, the question is: What kind of creep am I going to be? No matter how conscientious they are, the police officer and the soldier who kill in the line of duty, the professor who fails a struggling student, the parent who raises a hand to a child, the factory owner who fires a faithful employee, and the judge who must set a harsh sentence—all may have the feeling, not that they have made the right ethical choice, but rather that they have tried to make the least unethical one. Some roles may carry with them a shared sense that moral tragedy "goes with the territory." At the very least, measuring up to moral tragedy involves making a responsible

---

[10] Quoted in Chamberlain, "Legal Ethics," pp. 221–22.

[11] Sissela Bok, *Secrets* (New York: Pantheon Books, Inc., 1983), p. 120.

choice while appropriately acknowledging the magnitude of what has been sacrificed. It may require creativity and humility as well.

If there is a conflict between the obligation to keep one's oath of confidentiality and the obligation to come forward with evidence, then perhaps the core of the problem is with the oath itself. As Frank Armani said in Illinois, neither he nor his partner "had the slightest idea" of the oath's implications. Perhaps conscientious attorneys should not take such oaths. In his extensive critique of professional ethics, Alan Goldman has written:

> If I have promised a friend to aid him in some immoral end . . . , then the fact that I later refuse the aid does not entail that I have wronged my friend. I should never have made the promise in the first place, knowing that the fulfillment of it would have morally objectionable results; and, having made it, I should not now fulfill it. My friend or a third party might reasonably complain at my having made the promise, but not at my having failed to keep it.[12]

Goldman says that "a simple disclaimer at the beginning could avoid completely the intrinsic wrong of a breach of trust later on." Similarly, in her treatment of professional secrecy, Sissela Bok writes:

> To invoke a promise, therefore, while it is surely to point to a *prima facie* ground of obligation, is not to close the debate over pledges of secrecy. Rather, one must go on to ask whether it was right to make the pledge in the first place. . . .[13]

Her view, like Goldman's, is that there are some promises of confidentiality that professionals should not make.

Goldman and Bok seem to accept that a pledge of confidentiality can create a morally tragic situation. And their insight—that the most productive way to deal with such dilemmas is to work to prevent their arising—is an important part of ethical competence, especially for attorneys. But at the same time their analysis shows that Armani's oath is really not central to the question of lawyer-client secrecy. The issue is moved back one step, so to speak, to the separate question of whether lawyers should take such oaths in the first place. If we know (as Bok and Goldman seem to think we do) that the oath commits lawyers to unethical courses of action, then there is a good reason for lawyers to revise the oath. At best, only qualified promises of secrecy are permissible. If the oath is not revised, then, and if Bok and Goldman are correct, men and women who are concerned about conscience should refrain from becoming lawyers. Those who have taken such oaths and so committed themselves to unethical courses of action have been morally imprudent, opening

---

[12] Alan Goldman, *The Philosophical Foundations of Professional Ethics* (Totowa: Rowman & Littlefield, 1980), p. 135.

[13] Bok, *Secrets,* p. 121.

themselves to moral tragedy. But are Goldman and Bok correct in judging that the oath commits lawyers to unethical conduct? This we must soon consider.

There is another reason why the oath is not central to the question of lawyer-client confidentiality. Priests take a sacred oath pledging to keep secret the confidences of the confessional. But suppose that, because of a missed ritual and a bureaucratic mishap, someone is admitted to the priesthood without having taken the oath. Suppose it were this priest who had taken confession from Garrow and who knew where the bodies were buried. If the oath were the central reason for confidentiality, then, having not taken the oath, this priest would be completely free to hail the first police officer and have the penitent Garrow arrested. But this seems intuitively wrong; it suggests that the oath of confidentiality is a ritual *acknowledgment* of the professional's obligation—a solemnizing of it—rather than the source of it. It suggests that it is *being a priest, lawyer, or doctor* that is the ground of the obligation of confidentiality and that the roles themselves carry with them the expectation and understanding that the persons occupying them can be trusted. If attorneys should acknowledge a duty to keep secret their clients' communications, then that is a reason for including such a provision in ritual pledges taken upon entry into the profession. If attorneys shouldn't acknowledge any such duty, the oaths should be changed accordingly. Why then should such a general duty be acknowledged?

POINTS OF HONOR

David Mellinkoff has suggested[14] that the historical roots of the obligation of confidentiality are entwined with a certain ideal of gentlemanly honor. Lawyers are supposed to be gentlemen, and a gentleman is one who can be trusted: He who would reveal a confidence is no gentleman. E. M. Forster, in a well-known remark, has underscored the seriousness of this point of honor: "If I had to choose between betraying my country and betraying my friend, I hope I should have the guts to betray my country." It is difficult to say whether the ideals and commitments involved in friendship are more important than those involved in citizenship; it is difficult to defend a clear criterion for deciding which should give way when there is conflict.[15] Loyalty seems to be built into the very concept of friendship. In betraying one's friend, one abandons the relationship of friendship: "I thought we were friends," or "I thought you were a gentleman." In one's choices of action, one defines oneself.

Mellinkoff remarks that the right to speak with another in private is a mark of a

[14] David Mellinkoff, *The Conscience of a Lawyer* (St. Paul: West Publishing Company, 1973), pp. 134–40.

[15] Carol Reed's 1949 film, "The Third Man," is a sensitive exploration of such a dilemma. Joseph Cotten plays a writer whose old friend, played by Orson Welles, has become an arch-criminal. The writer must decide whether to remain loyal to his friend or to use his "friendship" to help the police bring the criminal to justice.

free man.[16] And it is the roles of gentleman, friend, etc., that make it possible to rest assured that one won't be betrayed. Bruce M. Landesman has sensitively described the value of confidential relationships:

> [The] dual nature of confidentiality can be understood in a somewhat metaphorical way: when a speaker delivers information in confidence, the speaker attempts to make the hearer a part of his own self, his "extended self," with respect to the information revealed. He needs the hearer to be another person, another "ear" and mind who can register his information and respond to it; "revealing" a confidence to a wall or a dog is no substitute for telling a person. At the same time, he needs the hearer not to be another person, but to be a part of his own self so that the information will not be used except as he chooses. Dropping the metaphorical notion of an extended self, the idea is that with respect to the piece of information revealed, the hearer is not free to use it as an autonomous moral agent. The information, in effect, still "belongs" to the speaker who would not have "lent" it unless he knew he could retain control of it. I suggest that both the speaker and hearer in a situation in which information is imparted in confidence perceive the situation in this way or at least realize that this is how it is supposed to be perceived.[17]

In Jeffrey H. Reimann's view, such control over information about oneself, and, more generally, the important social value of privacy, is not simply important to the flourishing of a healthy self; it is necessary for selfhood itself.

> *Privacy is a social ritual by means of which an individual's moral title to his existence is conferred.* Privacy is an essential part of the complex social practice by means of which the social group recognizes—and communicates to the individual—that his existence is his own. And this is a precondition of personhood. To be a person, an individual must recognize not just his actual capacity to shape his destiny by his choices. He must also recognize that he has an exclusive moral right to shape his destiny. And this in turn presupposes that he believes that the concrete reality which he is, and through which his destiny is realized, belongs to him in a moral sense.
>
> *And* if one takes—as I am inclined to—the symbolic interactionist perspective which teaches that "selves" are created in social interaction rather than flowering innately from inborn seeds, to this claim is added an even stronger one: privacy is necessary to the creation of *selves* out of human beings, since a self is at least in part a human being who regards his existence—his thoughts, his body, his actions—as his own.[18]

Reimann's analysis can account for the moral indignation we feel when we learn that others have read our mail or eavesdropped on our telephone conversations. It helps to explain the outrage we feel toward crimes such as rape and kidnapping. The need for a measure of control over how we are experienced by others can thus provide a powerful justification for social respect and protection for special rela-

---

[16] Mellinkoff, *Conscience of a Lawyer,* p. 137.

[17] "Confidentiality and the Lawyer-Client Relationship," 4 *Utah Law Review* 775 (1980).

[18] "Privacy, Intimacy, and Personhood," *Philosophy and Public Affairs* 6 (1976): 26-44.

tionships of trust and confidence.[19] The interest in such a protected relationship is especially strong for those like Garrow who need to understand their legal situation and options. Thus the "friend," the "gentleman," or the lawyer who reveals a confidence violates the basic ethical principle of respect for persons and compromises the correlative social ideal of the dignity of the individual. Just as it would be wrong to use torture or threats of harsh treatment to force Garrow to incriminate himself, so it is equally wrong to uncover his secrets by gaining his confidence under false pretenses. What one can't do by force, one cannot do by fraud either.

But there is a ready reply to this putative justification for lawyer-client confidentiality. In the Lake Pleasant case we are not dealing with an ordinary violation of privacy—eavesdropping on innocents, for example. Garrow has raped and killed and, in so doing, has violated the dignity of the individual about as much as it is possible to violate it. Having denied minimal respect to another, Garrow cannot consistently claim such respect for himself. He has thus forfeited his right to his measure of control over how he is experienced, his right to have his attorney withhold the evidence of his crime from others. The obligation to respect the moral space of others does not apply when the right to such respect is forfeited.

Though this objection has strong emotional appeal, it will not stand. While it is true that, having raped and killed, Garrow cannot consistently claim that he should not in turn be raped and killed, it does not follow from this that each of us is morally free to rape and kill Garrow. While this may be tolerable in a vendetta culture where there is no legal system, it won't do where there is a shared commitment to law and due process. When important rights are lost, the forfeiture must occur in accordance with appropriate legal procedures. Garrow may somehow deserve to forfeit privacy, social respect for his dignity as a human being, and forms of loyalty that he would otherwise enjoy. But that forfeiture, should it occur, must be in accordance with procedures that will ensure due deliberation and fairness; it must not be at the whim of his court-appointed attorney. Though it may be proper for Garrow's rights to be forfeited in accordance with law, it is improper for attorneys to preempt the process entirely on their own.

In fact, even defendants who are convicted—not, like Garrow, merely accused—of the most serious crimes do not forfeit the right to a relationship of trust and confidence with an attorney. We do not punish criminals by denying them legal counsel. Even when we execute convicts, up until the final moments the right to counsel is secured and respected.

---

[19] Erving Goffman, one of the "symbolic interactionist" sociologists cited by Reimann, has used the expressions "territories of the self" and "the private reserve of the individual" to focus on the general idea that Reimann develops. See *Asylums* (New York: Anchor Books, 1961), pp. 23, 29. It is a characteristic feature of totalitarian governments and what Goffman calls "total institutions," such as prisons and insane asylums, that, within them, respect for the boundaries of such private space is substantially diminished.

QUALIFIED CONFIDENTIALITY

A second, somewhat more sophisticated response might appear more promising. It is not that the client's right to privacy is forfeited; it is that other social interests militate in favor of limiting the obligation of confidentiality. As Bok, Goldman, Landesman, and others have argued, lawyers should not make any blanket commitment to keep their clients' secrets. They should leave open their option to reveal some things if it turns out that these ought to be disclosed. Within the framework of this general objection, two positions are possible, each of which is an alternative to what we will call "unqualified confidentiality"—the position that attorneys should make and keep blanket promises of confidentiality.

The first alternative, which we will call "discretionary confidentiality," holds that lawyers should make no promises of confidentiality whatever. Since it can always come about that important social interests will necessitate disclosure, clients should be forewarned that anything they say may be used against them. Of course the attorney can promise not to reveal client communications unless there is a good reason, and can list reasons that have seemed good in the past. But when the client speaks, there will be an ineliminable risk that the lawyer will disclose. Lawyers must be discreet, but they should not limit their autonomy in ways that may bar them from doing right later on. Discretionary confidentiality essentially removes the question of disclosure from the domain of professional ethics, permitting the attorney's personal standards and ideals to be controlling. It means, in essence, that there may be as many ways of drawing the line as there are attorneys. While such an arrangement may be appropriate where attorney and client know a good deal about each other—as when they are close friends or come from similar backgrounds—under other circumstances discretionary confidentiality would appear to create more client apprehension than necessary.

The second position, which we will call "qualified confidentiality," accepts that a qualified promise of confidentiality is both desirable and possible and that clients are entitled to know in advance when they can expect the obligation of confidentiality to protect them and when they cannot. Lawyers collectively, as a matter of the profession's ethics, must carefully specify the conditions under which confidentiality will not apply. Only then can they do good work while avoiding moral dilemmas and accusations of betrayal. The client's interests in privacy and autonomy will be protected, but only within a domain that is circumscribed by the profession to take into account the social interests that attorneys, like all citizens, should respect. Our discussion will focus on this second position calling for an explicitly qualified acknowledgment of confidentiality.

What would some of these counterbalancing social interests be? In the Lake Pleasant case we might want to allow for the social interests in solving the mystery of Susan Petz's disappearance, in the burial of her body, and in the conviction and punishment of her murderer. Some critics urge disclosure of dangers to others and disclosure of client intentions to commit crime, particularly perjury on the witness stand. (Neither one of these would apply in Garrow's case.) Others have developed hypothetical cases involving threats to national security and situations in which an innocent person would otherwise be executed. The general idea is that, in so attenuating the obligation of confidentiality, social harms will be prevented and social goods will be promoted. Though the client's autonomy and privacy are important, they are outweighed by other social interests which the attorney must respect.

If the attorney's obligation of confidentiality is explicitly qualified, the oath taken upon entry into the profession (and any promises of confidentiality given to clients) will have this general form: "I promise to keep secret all client communications unless revealing them will promote G, where G is some social good, or prevent H, where H is some social harm." The profession must fill in the blanks by specifying as carefully as possible the social goods and harms that will require disclosure.

From the client's perspective, qualified confidentiality will mean that care must be taken in speaking with an attorney. The lawyer must reveal certain types of information to others who may then use it to the client's detriment. We may suppose that people in general want to avoid punishment. That they do is part of our reason for imposing punishment; and, in general, it is also the reason why criminal defendants seek out the assistance of attorneys. Since punishment is feared, people will usually not feel free to share with attorneys information that their attorneys may reveal and that others may subsequently use to sustain criminal charges against them. Thus any qualification of the obligation of confidentiality must have as a consequence that clients will not be so free to discuss their situation with legal advisors. And, because fearful clients will withhold information, lawyers will not know what the clients have done and consequently will not be aware of the legal risks. Since in these cases lawyers will be in the dark about critical information, they will be less effective in counseling and representing their clients.

There can be little doubt that the greater the client's fear that the lawyer will disclose, the more difficult it will be for attorneys to develop a relationship of trust and confidence. Qualified confidentiality interferes with client openness and thus the ability of those in the legal profession to do their best work. While it may be that it is necessary to qualify confidentiality if certain social goods are to be promoted and certain social harms prevented, it appears that at least one social good is compromised by so limiting the attorney's obligations.

Critics of confidentiality and attorney-client privilege have admitted but downplayed this concern. Jeremy Bentham, in his *Rationale of Judicial Evidence,* strongly attacks the privilege that immunizes an attorney from the liability to testify when a client "has confessed his delinquency, or disclosed some fact which, if stated in court, might tend to operate in proof of it. . . ."

> But if such confidence, when reposed, is permitted to be violated, and if this be known (which, if such be the law, it will be), the consequence will be, that no such confidence will be reposed. Not reposed?—Well: and if it be not, wherein will consist the mischief? The man by the supposition is guilty; if not, by the supposition there is nothing to betray: let the law advisor say everything he has heard, everything he can have heard from his client, the

client cannot have anything to fear from it. That it will often happen that in the case supposed no such confidence will be reposed, is natural enough: the first thing the advocate or attorney will say to his client, will be – Remember that, whatever you say to me, I shall be obliged to tell if asked about it. What, then, will be this consequence? That a guilty person will not in general be able to derive quite so much assistance from his law advisor, in the way of concerting a false defense, as he may do at present.[20]

In similar remarks, Goldman argues for disclaimers that would warn clients of the limits to the ethical obligation of confidentiality:

Would such disclaimers have morally disastrous effects? They might cause guilty clients to try to hide their guilt or to omit certain incriminating facts in their accounts to their lawyers. But if a client is guilty, then it is not so troubling that he might want to hide this from his lawyer. If he is innocent, the lawyer should still be able to convince him that it is best for the lawyer to know all incriminating facts in advance in order to defend him effectively.[21]

But the arguments of Bentham and Goldman presuppose that those who are as pure as the driven snow will know that their conduct is legally unassailable and that those who have crossed the margins of legality will know of their vulnerability to judicial action. In very simple legal systems with good mass legal education programs, this may be so. But in complex, professionalized systems, judgments of guilt may be highly technical. Laymen cannot be expected to know about such matters as the applicability of defenses and the admissibility of evidence. Monroe Freedman has argued for the importance of trust in the attorney-client relationship, stressing that clients may withhold exculpating evidence out of a fear that it is incriminating.

[O]ne client was reluctant to tell her lawyer that her husband had attacked her with a knife because it tended to confirm that she had in fact shot him (contrary to what she had at first maintained). Having been persuaded by her attorney's insistence upon complete and candid disclosure, she finally "confessed all"–which permitted the lawyer to defend her properly and successfully on grounds of self-defense.[22]

Michael Bayles draws another fable from the lore of the legal profession.

Clients . . . might not fully appreciate the significance of facts. This . . . is dramatically illustrated by an old lag convicted of burglary and appearing before a judge for sentencing at the Old Bailey in London. When the judge

---

[20] Jeremy Bentnam, *Collected Works* VII, edited by J. Bowring (Edinburgh: Tait, 1827), p. 474.

[21] Goldman. *Philosophical Foundations of Professional Ethics*, p. 136.

[22] Monroe Freedman, *Lawyers' Ethics in an Adversary System* (Indianapolis: The Bobbs-Merrill Company, Inc., 1975), p. 4. Much of my analysis of the obligation of confidentiality parallels Freedman's. I have also found helpful an unpublished article by Mark A. Wicclair on confidentiality in journalism: "A Shield Right for Reporters v. The Administration of Justice: Is There a Conflict?"

asked him whether he had anything to say before being sentenced, the man replied that it was unjust and unfair that he be sentenced for the crime, that he was completely innocent, and that he could prove it. The skeptical judge inquired how he could prove it. The man responded that he could not have done it because he was in prison on the day the burglary occurred. When the startled judge asked why he had not mentioned this before, the defendant replied that he thought the jurors would have had a poor opinion of him if they knew he was an ex-convict. To obtain as much information as possible from clients, professionals need to assure clients that what they say will remain confidential.[23]

In short, it won't be just those who know of their legal vulnerability who will refrain from entrusting information to attorneys; it will also be those who fear that they may be vulnerable. That will include many whose conduct is, in fact, legally unassailable.

The United States Constitution evidences an appreciation of the way in which the technicalities of a legal system can perpetrate indignity upon a lay public. It is part of our "political morality" that citizens shall have the right to counsel in criminal proceedings. Since, as we have shown, full disclosure is necessary to the counseling process, and since citizens do not feel free to offer information if what they confide can be used to convict them, the right to counsel therefore implies an obligation of *unqualified* confidentiality on the part of the counselor. Qualified confidentiality says to a layman: You can remain silent and, in effect, give up your right to counsel, or you can get legal advice and run the risk that what you tell your lawyer will be used to put you in jail. In guaranteeing both the right to counsel *and* the right to be free from compelled self-incrimination, the Constitution protects people from having to make this Hobson's choice.

These observations show that with qualified confidentiality it will not just be the defendants who suffer. More important than that, it will be the quality of the judicial system itself.

But if qualified confidentiality incurs these social costs, what compensating weight is to be given to the benefits we will all enjoy if lawyers rush to reveal to others the disclosures of their client? When clients announce their intention to commit crimes, when they disclose impending danger to others, when they reveal where the bodies are buried, we are to suppose that attorneys will benefit us all by bringing forward this socially useful information. But as we have pointed out—and as Goldman and Bentham concede—the practice of revealing such information will have the effect of inducing clients not to disclose it. For a client to decide to reveal such information to an attorney who is openly committed to passing it on to the authorities is, in effect, for the client to decide to reveal it to the authorities. Now if a client is willing to reveal the information to the authorities, then the attorney's solicitude is hardly needed to preempt the decision. At the least, attorneys should be able to persuade wavering clients to disclose: Persuasion is supposed to be the

---

[23] Michael D. Bayles, *Professional Ethics* (Belmont: Wadsworth Publishing Company, Inc., 1981), pp. 84–85.

distinctive skill of the professional advocate. But if clients are unwilling to have the information revealed to the authorities, they will surely not confide it to attorneys who are sworn to disclose it. Either way, qualified confidentiality cannot be expected to contribute to the general welfare in the way its advocates suppose. Social benefits will not be promoted and social harms will not be prevented by attorneys who convey client information to the authorities. This is because, without promises of confidentiality, these clients will not disclose the socially useful information to their attorneys in the first place.[24]

But qualified confidentiality will bring about another loss as well. For under unqualified confidentiality, clients will feel free to disclose everything to their attorneys, at least insofar as pledges of secrecy can make it so. And, though attorneys will not be free to compromise their clients' interests by revealing their secrets, they can still counsel their clients to allow socially useful information to be disclosed, and they can try to persuade clients to give up illegal or unethical plans of action. Admittedly, lawyers will not often succeed in these efforts, but sometimes they will. If, however, clients do not reveal the information or their plans to their attorneys, then society will lose whatever benefit it now derives from lawyers who succeed in tempering antisocial intent. Thus, not only will the public not be better off if lawyers routinely divulge socially useful information disclosed by their clients (such information will not be disclosed to lawyers in the first place); under qualified confidentiality, socially useful counseling that attorneys now are able to offer will be impossible and the public will be worse off, at least to the extent that such efforts now succeed. It may be that the legal profession has a responsibility to help civil authorities. But certainly not when that help is illusory and not when it undercuts the capacity of the profession to meet its primary responsibilities.

THE LAWYER'S MORAL PERSONALITY

Bruce M. Landesman has argued that attorneys bear weighty moral burdens in meeting these responsibilities. Worrying about a troubling aspect of the lawyer's commitment to confidentiality, he has written:

> [I]f the case for disclosure were based solely on consequentialist considerations, the case would not be very strong. But something else is involved, the lawyer's own moral status and worth. If disclosure is not allowed, the lawyer will sometimes be in a position of permitting something quite evil to happen. The policy of disclosure will avoid or minimize this. I think that no one

---

[24] It is sometimes said that there is no empirical evidence that people will keep their incriminating secrets in the absence of an expectation of confidentiality. Thus, for all we know, Bentham and Goldman might well be wrong in thinking that clients will not disclose potentially damaging information if lawyers cannot pledge secrecy. But it should not be surprising that there is no hard data on the number of incriminating secrets that are kept: only the ones that are revealed can be tallied. Methodologically, the statistical study of guilty secrets is plagued by enormous difficulty. That leaves us only with motivational arguments of the type developed in the preceding paragraphs.

should be forced or required by social rules to stand by while genuine evil occurs; the damage to one's moral personality is unacceptable (and possibly habit-forming). My conclusion is that this important concern for the lawyer's own moral status and worth is weighty enough to make the case for disclosure stronger than the case against.[25]

It is not quite accurate for Landesman to say that unqualified confidentiality will require lawyers to "stand by" while genuine evil occurs. Their inability to take a particular very effective course of action does not entail that nothing can be done. Other potentially fruitful courses can surely be tried. Still, a lawyer may end up "permitting something quite evil to happen" because he or she will not breach a trust. And Landesman is right in stating that disclosure will minimize this. But what exactly is "this"? The policy of disclosure will not minimize the genuine evil but only the individual attorney's *knowingly standing by* while it occurs. More "genuine evil" will occur under qualified confidentiality. But it will be the legal profession collectively that is standing by when it could do something to prevent some of it; it won't be an individual lawyer who may do anything short of betrayal to prevent the evil.

Consequentialist considerations aside, Landesman contends that damage to the lawyer's moral personality is so great in these cases that disclosure must be permitted for the attorney's sake. He appears to be wondering, as did the mother of Susan Petz, how anyone could "live with such a thing." But if Landesman is correct about the damage to the attorney, it does not follow directly that lawyers should disclose. If, as I have argued, unqualified confidentiality is required if attorneys are to meet their responsibilities in a sophisticated legal system; and if, at the same time, Landesman is correct in stating that no one can be ethically prohibited from intervening as required to prevent genuine evil from occurring, then it follows, not that attorneys should break confidences, but rather that no one should enter the legal profession. More strongly, it follows that the good society will be one without lawyers.

But is it necessary that the moral personality of the attorney suffer under unqualified confidentiality? The anguish that attorneys experience while endeavoring to come to terms with these dilemmas may reflect a failure adequately to understand the special obligations of the profession and their justification. It may be the product of an errant conscience.

If, as I believe, the preceding justification for unqualified professional confidentiality is sound, then it would seem to follow that there are some things (betraying confidence, for example) which it is not permissible for lawyers to do in order to prevent genuine evil from occurring. It would appear that it is ethically permissible to become a part of a collectivity which, on balance, will reduce the amount of genuine evil that is done even though, for some specific evils that might otherwise have been prevented, members must knowingly let these evils occur. These moral

[25] "Confidentiality and the Lawyer-Client Relationship," in David Luban, ed., *The Good Lawyer* (Totowa: Rowman & Allanheld, 1984), pp. 208-9.

principles do not seem unreasonable. The central issue is not whether attorneys will be ethically troubled while endeavoring to live up to the standard; it is rather whether they will be ethically culpable. The central issue is whether or not the professional standards are sound. Surely it would make the burdens easier to bear if those in the legal profession commenced discussion on the possible personal toll being taken by the practice of professional confidentiality. If a characteristic type of damage does occur to the lawyer's moral personality, perhaps it can be mitigated in some way; through counseling, for example.

Still, even with a collective effort to alleviate the moral burdens that "go with the territory," anguish like Frank Armani's may be unavoidable. It is true enough that, for many, it will be difficult to measure up honorably to the standards of the profession. But nobody ever said it was easy to be a good lawyer.

Chapter 5

Complicity and the Limits of Zealous Advocacy

In sophisticated legal systems, lay clients need lawyers for two reasons: They need skilled professional advisors to help them to make decisions, and they need specialists to help them to carry out formal tasks. The fundamental responsibilities of lawyers are counseling and representation. In the preceding chapter we examined the lawyer's responsibility in counseling clients. We have seen that lawyers must provide legal advice if clients are to proceed knowledgeably in the context of a legal system that as lay persons they will generally not understand. The client has an important right, as do all citizens, to be apprised of the standards by which he or she will be judged. An advisor who is ignorant of the advisee's situation cannot give advice. Thus confidentiality is required if the injustices that would otherwise flow from ignorance of the law are to be minimized. In this chapter we consider ethical problems that arise in virtue of the attorney's responsibilities in representing clients. As with counseling and the professional obligation of confidentiality, representation and the professional obligation of "zealous advocacy" may require lawyers to act in ways that attract public criticism. It is difficult to discern how much of that criticism is deserved.

At the most basic level, the ethical problems of zealous advocacy are of two different types. In the first place, the course of action the client has decided to undertake may be improper in some sense. If the lawyer has an obligation to assist in the carrying out of tasks that are beyond the lay person's ability, the lawyer may become tainted or otherwise involved in the impropriety, whatever it is. At what point does an attorney begin to share in the guilt of the client's undertaking? We will refer to these as problems of complicity. In the second place, even where, broadly, the course of action decided upon by the client is unexceptional, it may be that there are improper as well as proper means of achieving the client's objectives. Given that attorneys are obligated to assist their clients, at what point does that assistance cross the boundary of acceptability? We will refer to these as problems of prohibited assistance. At a different level, both types of problem can become complicated by features of the institutional settings in which they occur. Even if we are clear that a certain course of action is culpably complicitous or that the assistance that is proposed is prohibited on its face, we may still be uncertain what weight should be given to other factors such as counterbalancing loyalties and responsibilities. These questions typically arise where attorneys have limited autonomy, as with an underling associate in a law firm or an "in-house counsel" for a large corporation. More dramatically these issues can arise where the concerns about complicity and prohibited assistance involve the lawyer's role within a systemically unjust legal system.[1]

In the criminal law, ethical problems can begin with the decision to represent. For every accused rapist, murderer, kidnapper, and extortionist; for every felon who is apprehended and brought to trial, there is an attorney endeavoring to clear the client of the charge. No matter how diabolically corrupt the defendant, no matter how fiendishly loathsome the offense, the attorney's professional responsibility will likely be to try to soften the judgment and mitigate the sentence as much as possible. It is possible broadly to distinguish between two different types of moral reservation about rendering assistance to the guilty (or, in civil cases, to those whose cause is not just). In the first place, the concern may be that, in discharging professional responsibilities, there is a risk that the attorney's moral character may be "tainted" by his or her systematic association with wrongdoers. The second reservation is that, in defending and assisting wrongdoers, the attorney is, ethically, something like an "accessory after the fact"; an accomplice, so to speak, in the wrongdoing itself.

THE TAINTING OF CHARACTER

Seymour Wishman's revealing book, *Confessions of a Criminal Lawyer*,[2] is an attempt to isolate and identify, autobiographically, the moral impairments—the "taintings of character"—that may be distinctive occupational hazards of criminal defense work. One of Wishman's characteristic concerns is with honesty.

> A criminal lawyer was surrounded by lies. Clients, witnesses, paid experts (such as psychiatrists), prosecutors—everybody—it seemed, lied or could be lying. Except me . . . most of the time . . . as far as I could tell. [pp. 36-37]
> The constant exposure to so many lies had made me suspicious of people. I had formed the habit of automatically sizing up character and trustworthiness, searching out motives. I had developed a reflex of recalling all inconsis-

---

[1] I have discussed one example of such systemic injustice in "Criminal Justice and the Negotiated Plea," *Ethics* 86 (1976): 93–106; reprinted in Kenneth Kipnis, ed., *Philosophical Issues in Law: Cases and Materials* (Englewood Cliffs: Prentice-Hall, Inc., 1975), pp. 304–318. The elimination of plea bargaining in El Paso County, Texas, is described by Judge Sam W. Callan in "An Experience in Justice Without Plea Negotiation," *Law and Society Review* 13 (Winter, 1979): 327–347; and in Alaska by Michael L. Rubinstein, Teresa White, and Stevens H. Clarke, *The Effect of the Official Prohibition of Plea Bargaining on the Disposition of Felony Cases in the Alaska Criminal Courts: Final Report* (Anchorage: Alaska Judicial Council, 1978). An interesting fictional account of a lawyer's efforts to eliminate plea bargaining is provided in a novel by James Mills, *One Just Man* (New York: Simon & Schuster, Inc., 1974).

[2] Excerpts quoted in this chapter are from Seymour Wishman, *Confessions of a Criminal Lawyer* (New York: New York Times Books, a Division of Random House, Inc., 1981). Copyright by Seymour Wishman. Reprinted by permission of the publisher.

tent statements, no matter how trivial. These were good habits for a criminal lawyer—if only they hadn't bled into my personal life. [p. 239]

. . . I had been conjuring up false emotions in an effort to influence the jury. I was suddenly, overwhelmingly aware of just how much these contrived emotions had been deceitful performances—calculated lies. Too many of the performances had been successful, and, as a result, I had been suspicious of my own emotions in other contexts. And certainly I had been suspicious of the emotions expressed by others for years. [p. 240]

Wishman is concerned about the degree to which criminal defense practice can fuel base motives.

. . . Through [my clients] I had become familiar with a world that would otherwise have remained hidden from me—a fascinating world, an intriguing, inviting, seductive demiworld. I remembered once asking a client about his heroin addiction, intrigued to find out what the heroin high was like. He clearly found such pleasure in it that he justified to himself giving up everything else to sustain it. He told me what he was giving up wasn't much—his life had been boring and depressing—and then he went on, rapturously, to describe how euphoric heroin made him feel. After my lengthy interrogation he asked, "Do you want some?" "No, I was just curious," I said, thoroughly shaken by the offer.

With little prompting, my clients would describe their lives in lurid detail— passionate, desperate lives filled with violence, drugs, and sex. I must confess I sometimes felt a vicarious excitement on hearing the exploits of these people so unfettered by the normal restraints. They were living and running on the razor's edge.

. . . I wasn't the only one titillated by the stories. Judges, prosecutors, detectives, jurors—virtually all those connected with the administration of criminal justice—experienced at one time or another this sense of voyeurism. [pp. 99–100]

Wishman's remarks are suggestive. He tries to trace the emerging deficits in his character to a professional role that both attracts and repels him. He appreciates how intoxicated he is by the thrills of criminal defense work, but at the same time is aware of the toll taken by his professionalism.

In an article mentioned earlier, "Lawyers as Professionals: Some Moral Issues."[3] Richard Wasserstrom hazards that certain special features of the lawyer-client relationship can render the attorney systematically amoral and, on occasion, even immoral. For, in Wasserstrom's view, lawyers occupy a simplified moral universe. (Recollect Lord Brougham's remark that the advocate "knows but one person in all the world.") For most of us most of the time, the interests of others ought to and do play a role in our deliberations about what we should do. But once an attorney has agreed to represent a client, there may be an overriding professional obligation to set aside concern for others and champion the interests of that one person. Being an attorney makes a big moral difference. Thus, for most of us, it may make a deci-

[3] Richard Wasserstrom, "Lawyers as Professionals: Some Moral Issues," *Human Rights* 5 (1975).

sive difference if it is pointed out to us that what we propose to do will mean, say, that a rapist will once again endanger others. But the rapist's attorney, within the framework of her role, is not supposed to take that consequence into account. The professional's concern must be for the client and not for the client's future victims. The interests of others don't directly figure into the equation. In a sense, this is the essential posture of the advocate.

Wasserstrom questions whether it is "a good thing for lawyers to be so professional," whether it is appropriate to consider "as morally irrelevant any number of factors which nonprofessional citizens might take to be important, if not decisive, in their everyday lives" (p. 8). There is comfort, even a seductiveness, in "being able to turn aside so many ostensibly difficult moral dilemmas and decisions with the reply; but that is not my concern . . . my job as a lawyer is to defend as best I can my client's interests" (p. 9). Even if, on balance, the lawyer's way of thinking is somehow justified, Wasserstrom worries that a high social cost is being paid, especially by the attorney.

> For to become and to be a professional, such as a lawyer, is to incorporate within oneself ways of behaving and ways of thinking that shape the whole person. It is especially hard, if not impossible, because of the nature of the professions, for one's professional way of thinking not to dominate one's entire adult life. [p. 15]

Wasserstrom suggests that the involvement of so many lawyers in Watergate was "the likely if not inevitable consequence of their legal acculturation" (p. 15).

Wasserstrom and Wishman notwithstanding, the evidence for the conclusion that legal practice—criminal and civil—can taint the moral character of the practitioner is far from conclusive. What evidence there is seems to be anecdotal, conjectural, part of the "lore" of the profession. And no one seems to be claiming that corruption of the spirit is an inevitability and that an honorable life in the law is ruled out by the very definitions of the terms. Still, because questions about moral character and virtue are a proper part of ethics, and because continued scrutiny of the issues here should be part of every profession's business (and every professional's business), notice has been taken of the issue. For many, perhaps most, the risks may be great.

THE FALSE PLEA

Once again we approach the defense of the guilty, but here from a different direction. Our concern now is not with the slow process by which character is corrupted, but rather with the immediate conditions for moral complicity in wrongdoing. Some might compare the attorney to the driver of the getaway car at a bank robbery. In removing the robbers from the scene of their crime, the driver does what he can to see to it that the criminals do not pay for their wrongdoing. How, one might wonder, is the attorney's "professional responsibility" any different? Though the suspects have been apprehended, the lawyer seems equally to assist wrongdoers in evading the just consequences of their actions. While the lawyer and the driver may be different in the eyes of the law, are they ethically distinguishable?

Let us look at questions of complicity as they might emerge in the course of a criminal case. Rodney Soames, the potential client, tells his attorney that he has committed the rape with which he has been charged. Following the crime, the victim, a Miss Margaret Gregor, called the police and gave them a rough description of her assailant. Among other things, he was said to be wearing a red and white striped sweater. Within forty-five minutes of the attack, Soames, wearing such a sweater, was spotted in the neighborhood and taken into custody. The following day Miss Gregor, a high-strung, emotionally distraught young woman, picked him out of a lineup. Except for saying that he was on his way to a friend's house and that he wanted to talk to a lawyer, Soames has told the police nothing. He is twenty-five, single, and steadily employed as a stock clerk.

Clearly one question that may arise is whether the attorney can properly take this client's case, undertaking to represent him as his advocate in the anticipated criminal proceedings. It is true that the attorney, if she accepts the case, will be "helping a rapist." But it is important here to distinguish between two senses in which one can help a wrongdoer. If what one does is to help a wrongdoer commit a wrongdoing, then one is clearly complicitous. But there are lots of ways in which one can "help a wrongdoer" that do not involve complicity in wrongdoing. If a convicted axe-murderer asks me for the time of day, I do not come to share in any guilt if I show him my watch. The same axe-murderer has a right to send a postcard and, accordingly, to have the assistance of officers of the postal service. Not only is it permissible for an officer of the postal service to give effect to the criminal's decision to mail the card; it would be manifestly improper for the official to refuse to do so. What needs to be shown is not that the attorney assists a rapist, but rather that she assists the rapist in doing something that is wrong. What is it, exactly, that the attorney will be doing for the rapist as the proceedings get under way? Only as we assess what is involved in legal advocacy on behalf of the guilty can we address the question of whether the attorney has overstepped the bounds of the ethical.

As the proceedings commence, the attorney's responsibility will be to see to it that her client, even if he is guilty, gets that to which the law entitles him. The Constitution guarantees to criminal defendants, regardless of their culpability, such important protections as the right to counsel, the right to due process, the right to present evidence on their own behalf, the right to cross-examine witnesses, the right to a public trial by jury, the right to appeal to the state for that which is guaranteed as a matter of law. In complex legal systems such as ours, this respect for the dignity of the defendant cannot be secured without skilled legal assistance. There are rules that the community sets for itself before it can properly punish one of its members, rules that secure for all of us a right to a fair hearing before the verdict is spoken. The defense attorney's job is, in the first place, to see to it that the community honors its own rules and, in the second place, to see to it that the court gets a chance to hear what can be said on the defendant's behalf.

It should be remembered that, in criminal proceedings, lawyers are virtually never in a position to do anything directly for their clients. Rather they request that certain things be done, they advance arguments, they petition. The ultimate disposition is always in the hands of another: the judge, the prosecutor, the jury, the appeals court, the warden, the governor. This is not to say that lawyers bear no responsibility for what these others do. Some responsibility is there. But it does serve to remind us that the petitions of legal representatives are but a part of a much larger decision-making apparatus involving judges, juries, prosecutorial adversaries, and a huge and complex body of law. The defense attorney's job is to see to it that that machine does not dishonor the community's own standards of fairness.

At the moment the chief problem is the arraignment. The client will appear before the judge to enter a plea of "guilty" or "not guilty." (No one is "innocent" in the American legal system.) Procedurally, the entry of the plea is the first formal step a defendant takes in the criminal process. If he pleads "guilty" to the facts, trial is essentially waived and all that remains is the sentencing. On the other hand, if he pleads "not guilty," then, unless the plea is later changed, the state will be "put to its proof" in the forum of a criminal trial. The prosecutor may be obliged to prove beyond a reasonable doubt that the defendant committed the crime for which he is charged. But now, since neither has looked at the state's evidence, it is not clear to the client or the attorney whether the prosecutor can meet the burden of proof. A crossroads has been reached and the attorney must make her first ethical decision: Should she assist the client in entering a plea of "not guilty"?

Perhaps the first answer that comes to mind begins with the observation that, since in this case to plead "not guilty" is to lie, and since it is wrong to lie, the defendant is prohibited from entering a plea of "not guilty." The rapist ought to plead "guilty" to the charge; after all, he committed the crime. Because it is wrong to lie—wrong knowingly to deny what is true—he should " 'fess up" and tell the truth. Accordingly, if what the lawyer and the client jointly undertake to do is to lie, it would seem that they are partners in wrongdoing at the very outset of the criminal process.

But is the rapist ethically culpable for a lie told in entering his plea of "not guilty"? Some would protest that a plea of guilty is not really an assertion at all. Rather it is more like what the starter does at a footrace in calling "Ready, set, go!" What the starter says, it can be argued, is not something that can be true or false. Rather it is a signal that certain things that it would be pointless or improper to do prior to the signal—running toward the finish line, for example—have now become appropriate. In a similar way the doctor's pronunciation of death is a signal that that which used to be the body of a person can now be treated as a corpse. Likewise a plea of "not guilty" signals that the charges will be contested and that a date for a formal trial must be set. The plea is therefore a move in a game, a mere legal formality, carrying none of the weight of a dishonest protestation of innocence.

But this rejoinder won't do. While it is true that the plea signals the applicability of certain procedures, it is equally true that the procedures have their applicability specifically because the defendant has denied committing the crime. The trial can occur precisely because there is disagreement (contradictory assertions) on the issue of whether or not the defendant committed the crime. As a society, we are committed to the principle that only the guilty should be punished. The defendant's guilt is the very reason for punishment. Since there are only two ways in which guilt can be adjudicated—either a guilty plea is accepted, usually before trial, or there is a verdict of "guilty" at trial—the terms "guilty" and "not guilty" do carry weight as assertions. To enter a plea of "not guilty" is to declare publicly "I didn't do it." If the declaration is false, we must regard the defendant as having lied. That a plea also serves as a key move in the criminal process does not entail that it cannot count as an assertion.

Some might protest that the plea cannot be counted as a culpable lie because it is not entered under oath. But while it is true that perjury, to be a crime, requires that the false assertion be one which is made under oath, it is not the case that non-perjurious dishonesty is innocent. The perjuror, it seems, lies twice: once in promising to tell the truth and a second time in the lie itself. The solemnity of the oath may also contribute to the culpability of the offense. But while we may have more reason to condemn the perjuror (who lies twice), we surely have some reason to be critical of those who lie, but less often.

Perhaps it can be argued that the plea of "not guilty" should not be condemned because, while the assertion is false (and known by the asserter to be false), it is not likely to produce false beliefs among those who hear it. An actor in a play may deliver the line "It is raining outside," but no one in the audience forms beliefs about the weather on that basis. While what he says may be false and, indeed, known to be false, the actor avoids culpability simply because no members of the audience can be expected to form false beliefs on the basis of what he says. Likewise, with the false plea of "not guilty," it may be equally unlikely that minds will be changed. The prosecutor, one supposes, has assembled evidence in support of the charge and has formed a responsible judgment that the defendant did indeed commit rape. When the defendant says "not guilty," it is not as if the prosecutor will sheepishly apologize for his mistake and drop charges. What we have when a plea of "not guilty" is entered is not so much a reason to form a judgment as a reason to withhold judgment until all the evidence has been weighed. Perhaps the false plea of "not guilty" is excusable just as the actor's false assertion is.

Still, it may be that the reason few take such protestations of innocence seriously is that we have come to expect defendants to enter pleas of "not guilty" in spite of guilt. Since we "know" that guilty defendants will often lie about their involvement in crime—to avoid punishment if for no other reason—they will not be credited when they declare their innocence. We do not exculpate known or suspected liars on the grounds that they cannot get away with their deception. If the reason why we don't believe defendants' assertions that they are not guilty is that we almost always have reason to believe they are lying, then the fact that we are not misled by their lies is not a reason for excusing the lies. It would thus appear that, even though no one is misled, a lie is told; and, insofar as lying is wrong, the defendant commits just such a wrong in his lie whether or not he succeeds in misleading others.

But is it clear that lying is always wrong? Cases readily come to mind in which, if we are not certain that a lie is justifiable, we are at least less than certain that it is wrong. Other important values can sometimes compete with honesty. An aunt asks us what we think of her hat. Must we speak our minds freely regardless of the effect on her sensibilities? Isn't it permissible, under the circumstances, to pretend? Absolutist positions on this issue are not uniformly persuasive. The standard philosophers' example involves a murderer who asks you if his erstwhile victim is at home. You saw your neighbor enter his house only moments earlier. It would appear that you should have both a right not to contribute to the enterprise of the killer and another right not to be threatened for refusing assistance. If, under the circumstances, the only way to secure these two rights is to lie, then perhaps the lie can be excused. Perhaps you can ethically lie to the murderer without incurring moral blame.

The correlative issue that emerges in the case of the criminal defendant's plea involves the obligation to assist officials in bringing oneself to justice. While the rapist cannot be excused from his crime, is he culpable as well for not cooperating with the officers of the criminal justice system in their effort to deprive him of his liberty? I think this is a difficult question. In part, the Fifth Amendment restriction on being compelled to testify against oneself is evidence of some sensitivity to the complexity of the moral issues here. At a minimum, if the defendant has other obligations that will be compromised by prolonged imprisonment—a condition that will likely be satisfied if he has any positive obligations at all—those obligations must be placed in the balance before we can judge whether the accused is culpable for not publicly acknowledging his guilt. If we suspect that the punishment meted out for the crime will be excessive or that the act, though criminal, was not a wrongdoing, then these considerations should also give us pause before we condemn anyone for hesitating before submitting to punishment. Moreover, loss of liberty is such a serious consequence that it may be necessary generally to excuse those who are not eager to embrace it. The point is that it can be a difficult moral question whether or not lying is permissible to avoid punishment. While we may revere the virtuous George Washington for confessing that he cut down the cherry tree, there may not always be an overriding duty to declare publicly one's wrongdoings when asked to do so. It may not be reasonable to expect everyone to measure up to George Washington's standard, especially when the punishment meted out is so much greater than the one he faced. Because of the consequences he faces if he confesses, it does not seem certain that the rapist is morally prohibited from falsely denying guit. And if we cannot say confidently that, all things considered, the rapist is morally obligated to confess his crime, then we cannot say confidently that the lawyer is unethical in assisting the rapist in entering a plea of "not guilty." Of course the lawyer does not herself lie in entering the plea on her client's behalf: "Your Honor, my client enters a plea of 'not guilty.' " It is worth observing that some legal systems—the system in the Federal Republic of Germany, for example— function without allowing for a "guilty" plea. There, the defense attorney's job is always to present the defense.

CONCERTING A FALSE DEFENSE

Let us suppose then that Rodney Soames will now stand trial for the crime of rape. The prosecution's chief witness is the victim, who claims to have gotten a good look at her assailant. She has told the police that the rapist wore a red and white striped sweater. Your client was picked up wearing such a sweater and was still wearing it when the victim identified him in the lineup. Such sweaters are currently popular attire; hundreds have been sold in the city. The young woman's identification may have been influenced by the fact that the distinctive sweater was not worn by any of the others in the lineup. Your client has shared with you the details of the rape and has told you that he was convicted on an assault charge eighteen months earlier in another state. The prosecution's case seems weak. There is the matter of the sweater, and, because of darkness in the woman's apartment where the rape took place and problems with the young woman's eyesight, the victim may not be a credible witness. There are no other witnesses.

In discussions with your client, you tell him that because the punishment for rape has recently been set quite high, juries have been reluctant to convict. However, they do seem to take a dim view of defendants who are unwilling to take the stand to give their version of what happened. Your client decides to try to lie his way to an acquittal, taking the stand and claiming that he has been incorrectly identified as the rapist; he was just innocently walking from his home to a friend's house when he was arrested by the police. Thinking that he stands a good chance of being believed by the jury, he wants to take the stand and lie under oath, thus committing the crime of perjury. Because of an air of innocence and believability about him, it seems to you that he is quite likely to get away with it. (Do you tell him this?) Though you have neither suggested nor encouraged perjury, he has come to his decision on the basis of the facts, opinions, judgments, and observations that his lawyer shared with him. He has been apprised of the punishment for perjury but elects to take his chances. How ought the defense attorney to deal with a client who intends to commit perjury?

If one looks back on what has happened, it may seem that the problem is rooted in the attorney's knowing too much. It is a widespread view that a criminal lawyer can better serve the client if he or she *doesn't* know what happened. Problems of complicity can be avoided if attorneys artfully arrange their relationship with the client to "preserve deniability" of knowledge concerning the offense. The classic statement of this approach is in Robert Traver's novel *Anatomy of a Murder*.[4] The lawyer is interviewing a client who is accused of first-degree murder.

> I paused and lit a cigar. I took my time. I had reached a point where a few wrong answers to a few right questions would leave me with a client—if I took his case—whose cause was legally defenseless. Either I stopped now and

[4] Robert Traver, *Anatomy of a Murder* (New York: St. Martin's Press, Inc., 1958): pp. 32–35.

begged off and let some other lawyer worry over it or I asked him the few fatal questions and let him hang himself. Or else, like any smart lawyer, I went into the Lecture. I studied my man. . . . He apparently did not realize how close I had him to admitting that he was guilty of first degree murder. . . . The man was a sitting duck. . . .

And what is the Lecture?

The Lecture is an ancient device that lawyers use to coach their clients so that the client won't quite know he has been coached and his lawyer can still preserve the face-saving illusion that he hasn't done any coaching. For coaching clients, like robbing them, is not only frowned upon, it is downright unethical and bad, very bad. Hence the Lecture, an artful device as old as the law itself, and one used constantly by some of the nicest and most ethical lawyers in the land.

The lawyer in the novel informs his client that if the facts are as he has stated them, there is no legal defense and he will probably be electrocuted. But, he goes on, if the client acted in a blind rage, there is a possibility of saving his life. He suggests that his client think it over. Not surprisingly, the client soon "recollects" the rage.

"Who, me? I didn't tell him what to say," the lawyer can later comfort himself. "I merely explained the law, see." It is a good practice to scowl and shrug here and add virtuously: "That's my duty, isn't it?"

But the cultivation and protection of the lawyer's ignorance are not consistent with the obligation of a counselor to get the facts. In its Standards Relating to the Defense Function, the American Bar Association condemns "the tactic, occasionally advocated by unscrupulous lawyers . . . of advising the client at the outset not to admit anything to the lawyer which might handicap the lawyer's freedom in calling witnesses or in otherwise making a defense." It is not just a question of what the attorney knows but, equally important, what the attorney should know. If, as was argued in the last chapter, counseling requires that attorneys try to find out what happened, they fail in their obligations as counselors if, preserving deniability, they ask the client not to tell them anything. Excessive concern for clean hands may therefore do more damage to professional integrity than excessive concern for the client. This is because lay clients cannot be expected to make judgments about which facts will help them and which ones will not.

In any event, Rodney Soames has already told his lawyer that he did it. What is the attorney's obligation now?

One option is to abandon the client. To put your client on the stand and build on his perjured testimony is to carry zealous advocacy too far. How would abandonment work? In criminal procedures, the bond between the attorney and the client can often be similar to that of a marriage: The court's permission must be obtained before the lawyer-client relationship can be dissolved. And, as with divorce, there may have to be good grounds for severing the tie. The attorney can go to the judge and ask to be removed from the case. Since getting a new attorney will take the court's time—justice delayed is justice denied—the judge will want to know the reasons. It is here that the attorney may face an insuperable difficulty. For she cannot explain her request by saying "My client wants to perjure himself on the witness stand" without letting the judge know that Rodney Soames is guilty. Apart from the violation of confidentiality, Soames cannot be expected to receive a fair trial in a courtroom dominated by a judge who has been told by the defendant's own attorney that the defendant intends to lie under oath about what he did.[5]

Maybe she can hint at the reason without disclosure. "Your Honor, I have an ethical problem with my client." But in practice this ends up being just as bad, for the words themselves are a clanging bell to experienced judges who will then be alert to what is going on. They will know what the lawyer is saying just because they know what the lawyer is unable to say.

In fact, even if we suppose that the attorney is able to withdraw from representation without compromising the judicial proceedings, that won't solve the problem either. For, knowing now how the game is played, the "innocent" and believable Mr. Soames will not make the mistake of telling the next attorney the truth.[6] The second attorney will rise in court to build on perjured testimony. However, he will not realize that that is what he is doing. And even if we were to require attorneys with "ethical problems" to resign and disclose the defendant's perjurious intentions to all subsequent lawyers, there would still be an ineliminable dilemma. For either some (unethical?) attorney will go forward to defend the perjurious Soames, thus perpetrating a fraud upon the court, or, if the bar is sufficiently "upright," no attoney will. If the former, we are back where we started; with his lawyer's assistance, Soames will get to present his perjurious case. But now suppose no lawyer will represent him. Let us suppose that all the lawyers who would have represented him have been disbarred. In that case, Soames cannot receive a fair trial, because the proceedings will not be fair in the absence of such legal representation. Because legal representation is required for a trial to be fair, and because no lawyer will represent Soames, the state cannot offer Soames a fair trial. Moreover, since, by its own rules, the state cannot properly punish people unless it offers them a fair trial; and since, because of a legal profession that refuses to defend Soames, the state cannot offer Soames the fair trial to which he is entitled, *the state cannot properly punish this rapist.* The ethics of the legal profession should not make it impossible for the state to punish the guilty. This is an equally unacceptable result.

---

[5] See *Lowery* v. *Cardwell* 575 F.2d 727 (1978).

[6] The second attorney would know if, as a condition of representation, he or she secures from Soames a waiver of confidentiality as regards communications from the first attorney. The first attorney could thus be required *by Soames,* her former client, to disclose all she knew to subsequent attorneys working on the same matter. The first attorney could also have a professional obligation to prevent former clients from defrauding and/or otherwise implicating in wrongdoing other subsequent attorneys who would not be aware of client deception. Such disclosure to a fellow officer of the court, solely to prevent a colleague from being unknowingly implicated in wrongdoing, is not a breach of professional ethics. Of course the disclosure should not go beyond second attorney(s).

BUILDING ON PERJURED TESTIMONY

So what is it like to build on perjured testimony? In the first place the attorney should work to discourage her client from committing the crime of perjury. She should tell him of the possibility that he will be found out and, if so, what the punishment is likely to be. She should advise him not to proceed with his plan. If she is unsuccessful in dissuading him, she may not then assist in the fabrication of his story. She may not suggest how the lie should be told. It would seem, however, to be acceptable to warn the client that some particular aspect of his story may permit the prosecutor to undermine his credibility upon cross-examination. But the lie itself must be the client's handiwork. At this stage, all the attorney owes to the client is the advice not to commit perjury and the assessment of what may happen if the defendant goes ahead anyway and lies under oath.[7]

The attorney will have to put Soames on the witness stand and let him speak. Obviously the questions that she asks her client must not signal in any way that the testimony is perjured. She may not sit back, for example, and ask him merely to tell his story if that is not how she would treat a truthful witness. Nor should she question her client in a way that might expose the perjury: That is the responsibility of the prosecutor. As Monroe Freedman has put it:

> . . . the criminal defense attorney, however unwillingly in terms of personal morality, has a professional responsibility as an advocate in an adversary system to examine the perjurious client in the ordinary way and to argue to the jury, as evidence in the case, the testimony presented by the defendant.[8]

---

[7] Though lawyers are legally prohibited from "suborning perjury," and though the Code of Professional Responsibility provides that lawyers shall not participate in the creation of false evidence, there is a thin line separating the giving of legal advice and complicity in the fabrication of the lie. There is a question, for example, about whether the attorney can recount the stories of defendants who have succeeded in persuading the court. I once spent a good part of a day listening to uncontested divorce proceedings, each lasting less than ten minutes. In every case—there were dozens—the complaining wife reported being struck on repeated occasions by her husband and, afterwards *in each instance,* rushing off to show her bruises to a friend. The friend was then put on the stand to testify that she or he indeed did observe the bruises on each of the aforementioned occasions. The overall effect was a bit like an audition, with different actors attempting common lines. It was the standard way unhappy couples got divorced in that particular jurisdiction.

Would it have been unethical for an attorney to discuss this script with a client couple who were no longer able to endure the legal bonds of matrimony? It is important that permissive principles not be extended too broadly. For the main argument here for coaching witnesses would be drawn from personal morality rather than professional ethics and would appear to be predicated on the existence of an oppressive legal system. As Chapter 2 should have made clear, the present work assumes that the system is defensible. Professional responsibility would militate in favor of collective action on the part of the legal profession to change the law. Indeed, in many jurisdictions "no-fault" divorce laws have been passed that obviate the pathetic charades of earlier years.

[8] Monroe H. Freedman, *Lawyers' Ethics in an Adversary System* (Indianapolis: The Bobbs-Merrill Company, Inc., 1975), pp. 40–41. In both this chapter and the preceding one, I am deeply indebted to the work of Freedman, whose arguments are echoed in much of my discussion.

This posture has attracted critics. For example, Sissela Bok takes issue with Freedman in her book *Lying*:

> If, that is, a lawyer has a client who lies to the court and thus commits perjury, Professor Freedman holds that his defense lawyer has the professional responsibility to ask questions which do not contest this testimony and even to use the false testimony in making the best case for the client to the court officers and the jury. That this can involve lying is beyond doubt. Nor is there serious doubt that such instances are not rare in actual practice. Yet perjury has traditionally been more abhorred than other lying. How is it, then, that it has come to be thus defended, albeit by a minority of commentators? Defended, moreover, not just as a regrettable practice at times excusable, but actually as a *professional responsibility*.[9]

In the first place, it should be plain that while perjury—lying under oath—would be committed by the client, it cannot be committed by the client's attorney, since, unless counsel takes the stand as a witness, what the lawyer says to the court is not spoken under oath. So Freedman cannot be said to advocate that lawyers commit perjury. Still, Bok suggests that, in endeavoring to make the best case for a perjurious client, a lawyer guided by commentators such as Freedman will lie in adverting to the testimony of the lying witness. Lies told to the court seem to be culpable, and Bok takes attorneys like Freedman to task for advocating such mendacity on the part of defense attorneys. But is mendacity a necessary part of responsible advocacy in cases such as this one?

In the Code of Professional Responsibility (Ethical Consideration 7-24) is contained the following admonition:

> In order to bring about just and informed decisions, evidentiary and procedural rules have been established by tribunals to permit the inclusion of relevant evidence and argument and the exclusion of all other considerations. The expression by a lawyer of his personal opinion as to the justness of a cause, as to the credibility of a witness, as to the culpability of a civil litigant, or as to the guilt or innocence of an accused is not a proper subject for argument to the trier of fact. It is improper as to factual matters because admissible evidence possessed by a lawyer should be presented only as sworn testimony. It is improper as to all other matters because, were the rule otherwise, the silence of a lawyer on a given occasion could be construed unfavorably to his client. However, a lawyer may argue, on his analysis of the evidence, for any position or conclusion with respect to any of the foregoing matters.

In the related Disciplinary Rules lawyers are warned that, in representing a client, a lawyer shall not "knowingly make a false statement of law or fact" (DR 7-102 [A][5]); and, even more strongly, in appearing in a professional capacity before a tribunal, neither shall an attorney assert "personal knowledge of the facts in issue, except when testifying as a witness" (DR 7-106 [C][3]). What this means is that if

---

[9] Sissela Bok, *Lying: Moral Choice in Private and Public Life* (New York: Pantheon Books, 1978), pp. 167–68.

there is some matter of fact that is to be determined by the court, lawyers involved in the case are prohibited from expressing as their own beliefs or as things known to them any personal statements concerning that matter. Not only are lawyers prohibited from lying on behalf of their clients: They have been traditionally *prohibited as well from asserting what they know to be true.*

In these passages the code is making an important and easily overlooked distinction between, on the one hand, advancing, on the basis of evidence presented to the court, an argument for conclusions that the attorney knows to be false, and, on the other hand, asserting the truth of those conclusions. If one studies the "assertions" of skilled attorneys, one will readily note the prevalence of such expressions as "I ask the jury to consider that . . ." or "I submit that . . ." or "The conclusion that must be drawn from this evidence is that . . . ," and so on. In criminal defense work, the task of the advocate is not, as Bok seems to suppose, convincingly to assert that the defendant is innocent: It is rather to present arguments for acquittal on the basis of the evidence presented to the court. Thus, in her summation, the argument presented by Soames's defense attorney could go as follows: ·

"As the jury in this case it is your solemn responsibility to reach a verdict. You have heard Rodney Soames tell his story, a story that the prosecution has been unable to refute. You must now ask yourselves whether you believe the defendant's clear explanation of what took place on that fateful afternoon, or whether you will accept the judgment of an emotionally distraught rape victim, rightly angered by the sexual assault committed upon her person, enraged at the man in the red and white striped sweater whom she dimly saw, without her glasses, in the shadows of her darkened apartment. You must ask yourselves whether, when she identified Rodney Soames in the police lineup only hours after her assault, she saw her assailant or saw merely an innocent bystander whose only mistake was to go to his job on that day dressed in the wrong clothes.

"Rape is a terrible offense, and the punishment for it is properly very severe. For that reason great care must be taken before tarring this young man with that broad brush. While it is true that the man who raped Margaret Gregor deserves to be punished, I submit that it is equally true that the prosecution has not proved that Rodney Soames is that man. I ask that, in issuing your verdict in this case, you tell the prosecutor and the police that, before they put anyone through the ordeal of a criminal trial, they make sure they can support their accusations with hard evidence. I ask that you find the defendant not guilty."

A careful reading of the lawyer's summation to the jury will not disclose any lies told by her to the court. Still, what Soames's lawyer says to the jury is, in a sense, wholly misleading. Soames has raped Margaret Gregor and his defense attorney knows it. She is arguing that the jury should form the judgment that Soames is not guilty when in fact she knows he is. In *ordinary discourse* when someone presents powerful arguments for the conclusion *P* (where *P* is some proposition), listeners are typically entitled to assume that the speaker believes *P.* At the least, listeners are entitled to feel wronged if they find out later on that the speaker knew all along that *P* was false. They are entitled to feel wronged even if line-by-line scrutiny of what was said fails to disclose a single materially false statement. It is not that lawyers lie; it is that, in this special way, they are dishonest.

But the problem with this criticism of defense attorneys is that it fails to take into account the degree to which language in a criminal trial differs from ordinary discourse. The jury in a criminal trial is not supposed to be taking what the defense attorney says as an assertion that the client is innocent. As has been noted earlier, what the attorney believes is irrelevant. Rather, the issue is whether or not the evidence adduced at trial supports, beyond a reasonable doubt, the proposition that the defendant committed the crime with which he has been charged. If juries and others are misled, it is not because defense attorneys are dishonest. It is rather because the required conventions of criminal defense work are insufficiently understood. Bok suggests (pp. 171–73) that judges should warn juries about this. Perhaps it is advisable that judges generally instruct those in the court that, if defense attorneys are unable to dissuade clients from lying under oath, they may be required knowingly to build upon perjured testimony. Judges should make it clear that, in undertaking to represent their clients, defense attorneys are not guaranteeing the truthfulness of what defendants say in court. And neither are defense attorneys supposed to let their personal beliefs about the client's guilt or innocence affect the manner in which they discharge their obligations of advocacy. Instructions such as these would seem ample to blunt criticisms of dishonesty.

LYING TO THE JUDGE

Having heard the arguments and the evidence, the jury finds Soames guilty of the crime of rape. In the interests of expediting sentencing, the judge asks Soames's attorney whether her client has any prior convictions. If Soames has no prior convictions, then it would seem appropriate for defense counsel to disclose this. To delay the proceedings might be to antagonize the judge. You don't want the judge to be deciding your client's punishment when he is angry at the defense. But, as we noted earlier, Rodney Soames was convicted eighteen months earlier on an assault charge in another state. And more to the point, the judge's question is completely improper. Other officers of the judicial system should have provided that information to the court in the form of a presentence report. The judge should not be relying on the defense attorney for information that may damage her client's cause.

At this stage four responses are possible. The attorney can answer the question truthfully: "Yes, your honor, my client was convicted on an assault charge." But here there is a betrayal of the client. Damaging confidential information is revealed to the court. The lawyer is no longer working for the client but for the court against the client. In the light of the arguments reviewed earlier on confidentiality in the criminal process, this answer seems unacceptable.

The attorney can refuse to answer the question. "Your honor, that is an improper question." Unfortunately, this answer may be equivalent to the first. If attorneys generally answer such improper questions when truthful answers will further the interests of their clients and refuse to answer them when the truth will damage those interests, then the judge will know (or at least have good reason to believe) that the client has a criminal record. The betrayal occurs as surely as if the attorney had spoken up directly.

A third response is to finesse the question. When asked, "Does your client have any prior convictions?" the quick-witted defense attorney can answer, "None that I can say, your honor." While judges may conceivably be misled once or twice by this dodge (and even this is unlikely), almost certainly the only one fooled will be the client. Experienced judges will be familiar with the gambit. The criticisms of the first two responses apply equally to this third.

The final response is to lie. "Your honor, my client has no criminal record." The justification for such deception is premised on the propositions that (1) the judge has no right that defense counsel provide him with this information; that (2) the information the judge is requesting is information that the attorney is obligated not to disclose; and that (3) all nondeceptive responses will have the practical effect under the circumstances of disclosing to the judge the very information that the judge is not entitled to receive from the attorney and that the attorney is obligated not to disclose. Under the circumstances it would appear to be obligatory for the attorney to lie to the judge.

But it may be unwise to hasten to this conclusion. For lying can be justified only if attorneys in general freely answer improper questions *when truthful answers are in the interests of their clients.* While it may not be open to Soames's defense attorney to see to it that all lawyers abide by a nondisclosure rule here, whether it serves their clients' interests or not, it is open to the legal profession to make such a determination. Suppose that the standard answer to such questions were something like this: "Notwithstanding whether or not my client has a criminal record, as a member of the legal profession I will face disciplinary proceedings if I proffer an answer to your inquiry. I respectfully ask that you withdraw the question without prejudice to my client." If attorneys routinely respond in this way, the case for deception cannot be made. The rule here is that if it is improper for attorneys truthfully to answer questions when the truth will hurt a client, it is equally improper to answer when the truth will help. This principle sets an important limit to zealous advocacy.

Chapter 6

Professional Responsibility
and the Distribution of Legal Services*

When goods of any type (including services) are distributed in society, a choice can be made whether they will enter the market to be bought and sold there, or whether they will be distributed or rationed wholly or in part in accordance with some principle other than the consumer's ability and willingness to pay the market price. Few would question that with respect to some goods—aftershave lotion, for example—market mechanisms are a reasonable and appropriate means of distribution. In their effort to maximize their profits, designers, manufacturers, and distributors compete with one another to produce the highest-quality goods at the lowest cost. Purchasers in turn make independent judgments about whether the goods offered for sale are worth their price. For some other goods, however—childhood vaccinations, secondary education, fire-fighting services—distributions are not nearly so dependent on transactions made between the end users of the goods and their suppliers. We can distinguish therefore between market systems of distribution and rationing systems, including in the latter category those systems in which ability and willingness to pay the market price for the goods are *not* the sole preconditions for receiving them.

In some cases, the justification for a rationing system involves an appeal to goals that are shared, more or less, by the community as a whole. We are all more secure when fires in our community are contained as quickly as possible. The public interest in speed and efficiency is not served if purchasers of fire protection services must negotiate with sellers while homes, businesses, and factories go up in flames. In a second category, the justification of rationing systems involves an appeal to some right. The arguments can be made that police protection services, legal services in serious criminal proceedings, and elementary education must be provided where the need arises, not merely because it is in the public interest that these be done, but also because the beneficiary of the good has some type of right, some entitlement to it. The victim who is being beaten up has a right to the assistance of a law enforcement officer. Those accused of criminal wrongs have a right to legal

*From Kenneth Kipnis and Diana T. Meyers, *Economic Justice: Private Rights and Public Responsibilities* (Totowa, N.J.: Rowman and Allanheld, 1985). Copyright by Rowman and Allanheld. Reprinted with the permission of the publisher.

assistance in proceedings that would be unfairly imposed in the absence of such help. And children have a right to be taught skills that are essential to a decent life in the complex society we will leave them.

In a third category of case—and it is one of these that will occupy us here—non-market mechanisms may be justified, not by an appeal to a right enjoyed by the beneficiary of the good, but rather by appeal to a duty or special responsibility assumed by those designated to provide the good. We may wish to say, for example, that where it is vital to their well-being, children should receive medical care, not because they have some kind of inherent right to health care (we may believe that no one has), but rather because, in becoming parents, mothers and fathers have assumed a responsibility to provide that care. The child is what lawyers would call a "third-party beneficiary."

In the United States, legal services in civil proceedings are for the most part made available through market distribution systems. To be sure, many attorneys and firms provide services at reduced fees or for no fees at all to people who might otherwise be deprived of needed legal advice or representation. Additionally, private organizations (the American Civil Liberties Union or the National Association for the Advancement of Colored People) and government-funded organizations such as the Legal Services Corporation also make available legal services without reliance on market pricing systems in distribution. In its state and national bar associations, the organized bar has played a role in the provision of legal services to those who cannot obtain them because of an inability to pay. While it is clear that legal services in civil matters have been made available outside of market distribution systems, there is doubt whether these services have been adequate to meet the general needs for them. But it will not be our purpose here to explore the dimensions of any such shortcomings. Rather, our chief concern will be to identify who it is who has central responsibility for the provision of such services, the form that such responsibility takes, and the grounds for that obligation.

Let us accept that our community has committed itself to an adversary system of adjudication. For the sake of the discussion that follows and as we argued in Chapter 2, we assume here that a public commitment to adjudication secures for each member of the community the following four rights: (1) the right to submit certain types of complaint to a judge or tribunal, (2) the right to have the other party to the dispute summoned to court to answer the complaint, (3) the right to have the judge make a decision in the case, and, if it is favorable, (4) the right to have the judge's decision enforced. Let us further assume that in an adversary system of adjudication responsibility for gathering evidence and marshaling arguments rests with the parties to the dispute. It is the judge's job, however, (1) to create a forum in which the parties can argue their cases, (2) to issue a decision in the case, (3) to appeal to or declare a rule applicable in all relevantly similar cases, and (4) to disclose the reasoning behind the decision. Finally, we assume that the overriding purpose of such a system is to make it as likely as possible that the judge's declaration of the rights of the parties will be a just decision and as likely as possible that it will be accepted by the parties to the dispute and by the community as a whole.

THE CONDITIONS OF INFORMATION AND EXERCISE

It would seem that for any legal system worthy of respect, the protection and support that the community provides for some should be made available to all whose claims are similar. To the extent that the community fails to make this protection available, it fails to provide equal protection: It fails to be just. Two conditions must be met if the protection afforded by legal rights is to be available to all with sound claims to it. First, it should be possible for citizens to obtain, at least generally, *information* about what the law requires or permits. There may be some cases, as when the law is unsettled, when only educated guesses are possible: Adequate authoritative information is not available because it does not exist. To be sure, even when rights are problematic, a commitment to adjudication secures for members of the community a right to an authoritative clarifying judgment in the event of a dispute. But when information does exist, it should be possible for a member of the community to find out what the legal standards are. Legal rights have little value (and legal obligations can be unfairly perilous) to those who cannot find out which ones they have.

Second, when members of the community have a legal right to something that has been denied to them, it should be possible for them to obtain whatever protection and support the community guarantees to them as a matter of law. In other words, it should be possible for them to *exercise* what rights they have. Thus if Potter has the legal right that Watson not build the tall orange fence on the boundary separating their two lots, it should be possible for her to commence some community-constituted process that will have as its effect the rectification of Watson's wrong. Potter might be able to invoke some legal requirement that Watson remove, relocate, or repaint his fence or that he compensate her for a continuing encroachment upon her interests. If the community is serious in its commitment to adjudication as a means of clarifying and securing legal rights for its citizenry, it must begin by securing generally for all citizens a right to information about what the law permits and requires, and a right as well to appeal to the law to secure that which the law guarantees to them.

Adversarial systems have the serious disadvantage that complaints may not be made and cases may be wrongly decided if the party in the right doesn't bring the case or loses it because of an inability to present intelligibly and persuasively what is, in fact, a solid case. Some citizens—let us call them nonparticipants—may be effectively excluded from the courts because of inadequate resources of one kind or another. Since the judge in an adversarial proceeding depends on the parties to do the investigative work and to present the results to the court in a useful way, serious injustices may be tolerated when they should not be or cases may be wrongly decided if one of the parties is unable to meet the requirements of adversarial adjudication. When this happens, the judicial system may serve generally to protect some perpetrators of injustice; may serve, in other words, to further injustice. Certain sectors of the community may be forced to put up with wrongs that the rest of us would not tolerate for an instant. Being unable to participate in the mechanism that the community provides for the settling of disputes, these persons will be exposed to wrongs without any prospect of legal recourse.

If such wrongs are to be rectified, measures will have to be taken that are outside the law. However, if in taking "direct action" wrongs are committed against those who are not similarly excluded from participation in the system, then the system will protect the victims of the nonparticipants in a way that it will not protect the nonparticipants when they are victimized. One thinks of the looting and destruction in America's periodic ghetto riots. Inquisitorial systems of adjudication seem not to have these same problems, since one official has the responsibility for doing the work of both sides, investigating the facts and interpreting the law. Injustice stemming from inequality in the resources of the parties is thus less likely to occur in these nonadversarial systems. If the community opts for an adversarial model, it must address this distinctive problem.

At the broadest level, adversarial legal systems can meet the conditions of information and exercise in several ways. Because each of these approaches ameliorates some difficulties while exacerbating others, they may be thought of as representing different agendas: With what kinds of problem do we wish to be occupied? The first solution is that of the "convivial" legal system.[1] In such a system care is taken so that people can generally be expected to understand their legal positions with respect to most matters and to be able to function within the legal system without assistance. This is brought about by (1) employing programs of mass legal education to ensure that virtually everyone has the knowledge and skill that are needed, and (2) opting for a simple legal system so that only minimal instruction is required.

The system can be kept simple by using a number of methods. Judges can be limited in the degree to which they are able to become specialists. They might receive only a small amount of specialized training, perhaps only after they are selected. And they could be rotated in and out of short single terms in office. Because in terms of training and experience judges would not be all that different from the litigants, courtroom discourse would not differ strikingly from the language of everyday life. Indeed, experience in the courtroom, as litigant and as judge, might be fairly commonplace among members of such a community. A convivial arrangement has the advantage that each person would know virtually everything anyone would need to know about the legal system: both what the law was on most matters and how to function in the courts. It would have the disadvantage—assuming this to be a disadvantage—that legal relationships and their derivative social institutions could never be so complicated as to require a specialist to understand what is involved in them.[2] Difficult-to-discern injustices might persist because the expertise required to identify and deal with them might not be developed. In essence, a

[1] I have taken the term "convivial" from the chapter entitled "Institutional Spectrum" in Ivan Illich's *Deschooling Society* (New York: Harper & Row, Publishers, Inc., 1972).

[2] For an illuminating description of a legal system that approaches conviviality, see Victor Li's account of the Chinese legal system in *Law Without Lawyers* (Boulder: Westview Press, Inc., 1978).

convivial system meets the conditions of information and exercise by means of mass legal education and simplicity.

On the other hand, the community could choose to make no effort whatever to educate the general public to the point at which it has an adequate understanding of the provisions of the law and the niceties of legal procedure. The legal system itself could be permitted to become as complicated as it may, with only highly educated and experienced specialists sitting on the bench. In such a "sophisticated" system, the ordinary person cannot be expected to understand his or her legal position with respect to many matters, and neither can the layman be expected to secure, all alone, what the law guarantees. In such a legal system, justice requires that there exist some mechanism for making available both information about the requirements of the law and skilled legal assistance. Without such a mechanism, a sophisticated legal system cannot be justified. Justice can thus require that a sophisticated adversarial system of adjudication be a "professionalized" system.[3]

SOPHISTICATED ADVERSARIAL SYSTEMS

Unlike the convivial arrangement, sophisticated legal systems do not provide for mass legal education, nor do they incorporate structural features that serve to limit the complexity of the system. Accordingly, in order to meet the conditions of information and exercise, they must provide for some sort of intermediary between lay persons and what will generally be a mysterious and intimidating legal system. There are three main approaches to the provision of such an intermediary: the free market, the liberal profession, and the public agency.

The Free Market

In the absence of mass legal education, judicial specialists create the need for lawyers. Just as—historically—shoemakers and repairers of appliances can materialize without invitation, so pettifoggers will appear about the courts to make specialized services available to those who have business there. In exchange for a fee, these self-designated attorneys will give legal advice, draft legal documents, and, with the court's permission, represent clients before the judge. It is important to note that these "protoprofessionals" differ greatly from what we now know as attorneys. For example, they will not have standardized educational experience, nor will they be certified in familiar ways. Though some may have been to "law school," completion of such a course of study will not be a prerequisite to the practice of law. Just as anyone can hold himself out as a gardener or as an automobile front-end specialist—and let the buyer beware!—so pettifoggers will fall all along the spectra of competence and integrity. There will be virtually no formal restrictions on entry into

---

[3] It is probably misleading to suggest that specialists are required because the system is complicated. While this has without doubt become true, a more adequate explanation would reveal that a system becomes complicated precisely because it is given over to specialists. This is not to say that complexity and sophistication are bad things; only that they create problems that need to be solved.

the field. Of course, some may not be able to earn a living in the legal-services business and will turn to other callings. Consumer services may alleviate some of the problems created by variations in quality, by selling information to potential clients about the relative merits of attorneys. Still, the purchaser of legal services will generally have no assurance (except for the word of the attorney) that the goods received are of their putative quality.

Should pettifoggers decide to organize, their distinctive form of society will be the "trade association," set up to further the economic interests of the membership. The trade as a whole may have problems that are best addressed by means of some kind of collective action. Perhaps too many people are entering the business, causing excessive competition and driving down the average income of the membership. Perhaps a few "rotten apples" have given pettifoggery a bad name and as a result there is a public-relations problem that needs attention. Perhaps programs can be set up that will help lawyers keep current on legal developments. A legal-services trade has the advantage that it may require little attention by the larger community. If disparities in financial resources are not too large among the citizenry, if the costs of litigation are not great, and if reliable information is readily available concerning the quality of practicing lawyers, the conditions of information and exercise can be met.

Sectors of the community that are without adequate legal services will almost naturally generate their own specialists as legal tradesmen seek out untapped markets. On the other hand, where poverty is significant in sectors of the community or where legal services are for other reasons not made available by market forces, the problems may be more difficult. Still, the protoprofessional lawyer may nobly offer legal services *pro bono publico* (for the good of the public). A sufficient level of such charity may serve adequately to address the community's concern to meet the conditions of information and exercise. It is important to note that pettifoggers would seem not to be under an obligation to do work for anyone except their paying customers. Appliance-repair services need not fix the electric mixers of those too poor to pay for the work. If the gratuitous charity of the legal trade will not suffice, the community can always decide to subsidize the purchase of legal services for those too poor to pay: It can provide "law stamps" on the model of food stamps.

The Liberal Profession

We noted in Chapter 1 that the development of a trade into a profession is a process and that occupations can be located at various points along the continuum. In American legal history, the process of professionalization can perhaps be said to have begun in 1870 with the organization of the Association of the Bar of the City of New York.[4] Samuel J. Tilden, addressing the first meeting of the first modern legal professional association, warned:

---

[4] R. Pound, *The Lawyer from Antiquity to Modern Times* 5 (1953), note 7 at p. 249. Pound describes the period between 1836 and 1870 as the "Era of Decadence" (pp. 223–49).

> Sir, [I] should not be unwilling that the Bar should combine to restore any power or influence which it has lost, except such power and influence as it may have deservedly lost. As a class, as a portion of a community, I do not desire to see the Bar combined, except for two objects. The one is to elevate itself—to elevate its own standards; the other object is for the common and public good. For itself, nothing; for that noble and generous and elevated profession of which it is the representative, everything.
>
> Sir, it cannot be doubted—we can none of us shut our eyes to the fact—that there has been, in the last quarter of a century, a serious decline in the character, in the training, in the education, and in the morality of our Bar; and the first work for this Association to do is to elevate the profession to a higher and a better standard. If the Bar is to become merely a method of making money, making it in the most convenient way possible; but making it at all hazards, then the Bar is degraded. If the Bar is to be merely an institution that seeks to win causes and to win them by backdoor access to the judiciary, then it is not only degraded, but it is corrupt.[5]

Tilden's language signals a new role for the bar, a new conception of the responsibility of lawyers, a striking departure from the idea of lawyering as a trade, and a commitment to the development of the liberal legal profession. The transition from something close to what we have described as a "free market" to the modern legal profession took many decades, but, as we noted in Chapter 1, the three critical steps in the process are roughly as follows.

First, practitioners within the trade begin to make a *claim to maximal competence.* Some lawyers, by virtue of superior training, education, and experience, exceed all others in knowledge and skill. An organization of practitioners within the favored class asserts a claim to speak for the whole class. And there is a criterion for deciding who belongs to the class and who does not. Because of the special knowledge and skill possessed by these practitioners, those outside the favored class lack the standing to judge the competence of these specialists. As the public comes to accept the profession's claim to maximal competence, it becomes reasonable to let the select class of practitioners certify and evaluate itself, excluding from practice those of dubious expertise. The favored practitioners, in association, stand ready to assume this responsibility.

Second, since in a society that is committed to a sophisticated adversarial system special legal knowledge and skill are vital to the achievement of justice, the process of professionalization requires that the profession make a *public commitment* to use its distinctive abilities in the realization of that significant social value. The profession pledges to give due attention to the special responsibilities it will assume in ensuring that the system of adversarial adjudication succeed in its task of justly addressing conflicts emerging within the community. We earlier noted the characterization of the legal profession in the American Bar Association's Code of Professional Responsibility: "Lawyers, as guardians of the law, play a vital role in the preservation of society. The fulfillment of this role requires an understanding by lawyers of

---

[5] Quoted in R. F. Marks, K. Leswing, and B. Fortinsky, *The Lawyer, the Public, and Professional Responsibility* (Chicago: The American Bar Foundation, 1972), p. 13.

their relationship with and functions in our legal system. A consequent obligation of lawyers is to maintain the highest standards of ethical conduct." In characterizing itself as a guardian of the law, a guardian of the foundation of justice, the legal profession represents itself as dedicated to an ideal of social service; to "the common and public good" as Tilden put it.

Third and most important, the process of professionalization requires that the community recognize the favored members of the profession as the sole means by which legal skill and knowledge are to be applied. This exclusive *social reliance* on licensed attorneys is based on the preceding two stages. For if there is confidence that the favored members of the class of practitioners possess maximal competence in matters legal, and if there is trust that these same lawyers are reliably committed to the responsible application of their distinctive skills, then there will seem to be neither the ability nor the need to designate nonprofessionals as overseers of professional practice. As the profession secures trust and confidence, it takes control over the selection and training of candidates, the accreditation of professional schools and programs, the certification of new members, and the promulgation and enforcement of standards of professional conduct. It becomes an unregulated legal monopoly with respect to legal services, unauthorized practice being a criminal offense. In the end it is we citizens who, through representatives, delegate responsibility to professions or relieve them of it. Though permission to practice in the courts—admission to the bar—is initially granted by the judiciary, the privileges that lawyers enjoy can be ratified, extended, and revoked by legislatures.[6]

The Model Rules of Professional Conduct evidence a sensitive appreciation for the essential connection between the professional responsibilities of lawyers and the responsibilities of the legal profession. Its preamble contains the following:

> To the extent that lawyers meet the obligations of their professional calling, the occasion for government regulation is obviated. Self-regulation also helps maintain the legal profession's independence from government domination. An independent legal profession is an important force in preserving government under law, for abuse of legal authority is more readily challenged by a profession whose members are not dependent on government for the right to practice.
>
> The legal profession's relative autonomy carries with it special responsibilities of self-government. The profession has a responsibility to assure that its regulations are conceived in the public interest and not in furtherance of

[6] The New Mexico Supreme Court, in *Norvell* v. *Credit Bureau of Albuquerque, Inc.,* 85, N.M. 521, 514 P.2d 40 (1973), has recognized the following "indicia" of the "practice of law":

> (1) representation of parties before judicial or administrative bodies, (2) preparation of pleadings and other papers incident to actions and special proceedings, (3) management of such action and proceeding; and non-court-related activities such as (4) giving legal advice and counsel, (5) rendering a service that requires the use of legal knowledge or skill, (6) preparing instruments and contracts by which legal rights are secured.

These are typical issues for consideration in determining whether an individual is guilty of the unauthorized practice of law.

parochial or self-interested concerns of the bar. Every lawyer is responsible for observance of the Rules of Professional Conduct. A lawyer should also aid in securing their observance by other lawyers. Neglect of these responsibilities compromises the independence of the profession and the public interest which it serves.

It is helpful to compare the monopoly status of public utilities with the standing of the professionalized bar.[7] Corporations that operate as public utilities receive from the community an exclusive legal right to distribute some good or service within a defined geographical area. It is a great advantage to the corporation to have the assurance that it will not face competition; because of this, it may be able to keep its costs low and achieve economies of scale. From the point of view of the citizenry, however, the deal makes sense only if the corporation assumes the responsibility of providing reasonable service to all those within its area. As the United States Supreme Court put it in 1918:

> Corporations which devote their property to a public use may not pick and choose, serving only the portions of the territory covered by their franchises which it is presently profitable for them to serve, and restricting the development of the remaining portions by leaving their inhabitants in discomfort without the service which they alone can render.[8]

Without the commitment to provide service, the granting of the exclusive right to the corporation—the barring of all others from entering the market—does not make sense.

Likewise, in the absence of a commitment from the legal profession to provide service to all who need it, the granting of an exclusive right to the bar becomes a decision to exclude some sectors of the community from participation in the system of adjudication. Where only attorneys are permitted to advise and represent members of the community, but where no attorneys will agree to serve some community members with need for legal assistance, the community does not meet the conditions of information and exercise and is to that extent unjust. One mechanism for meeting the two conditions is a responsible legal profession. Its members would possess the knowledge and skill that the ordinary members of the community would lack. They would have an exclusive right to counsel and represent clients in legal matters. And finally, the profession as a whole would acknowledge its obliga-

---

[7] The characterization of the legal profession as a public utility has been developed by Marks and others in *The Lawyer, the Public, and Professional Responsibility*, pp. 288–93. Some of the key elements of their general view were developed decades earlier by Karl Llewellyn in "The Bar Specializes—with What Results?" *Annals of the American Academy of Political and Social Science* 167 (May 1933): 177–92; and "The Bar's Troubles and Poultices—and Cures?" 5 *Law and Contemporary Problems* 104 (1938).

[8] *New York and Queens Gas Co.* v. *McCall*, 245 U.S. 345, 351. On the ethical responsibility of public utilities, see Kenneth Sayre, ed., *Values in the Electric Power Industry* (Notre Dame: University of Notre Dame Press, 1977). See especially Chapter 3, Charles Murdock, "Legal and Economic Aspects of the Electric Utility's 'Mandate to Serve.'"

tion to serve adequately as the necessary intermediary between the public and an otherwise inaccessible judiciary. Thus the conditions of information and exercise are met through the legal profession's commitment to provide counseling and representational services.

Understood in this way, the liberal legal profession serves as an integral part of the legal system: Though they retain their autonomy, lawyers are *officers* of the court. Thus a serious failure of the legal profession is a serious failure of the legal system. The standards of practice that the profession as a whole imposes on its members must ensure that the counseling and representational services that must be made available if the legal system is to make sense are made available to the public in an adequate way.

Speaking through professional associations in codes of ethics, lawyers have acknowledged the bar's duty to serve all members of the community. Thus the first Ethical Consideration of the American Bar Association's Code of Professional Responsibility begins:

> A basic tenet of the professional responsibility of lawyers is that every person in our society should have ready access to the independent professional services of a lawyer of integrity and competence.

The legal profession, the collectivity of licensed attorneys, thus does provide a guarantee to the community as a whole that competent and responsible attorneys will be available to those who need them. Were it the case that large numbers of attorneys publicly disavow these representations made by organizations undertaking to speak on behalf of the profession, one would then have reason to doubt whether the public commitment expressed by the codes represented a public responsibility undertaken by the profession. But in the absence of widespread visible disassociation, one can only suppose that the codes express a commitment that is generally acknowledged. To be sure, the possibility exists, as Tilden foresaw, that the bar associations of today are merely yesterday's trade associations with improved public relations programs. And it may be that the codes are not intended—perhaps were never intended—to bind lawyers to responsible levels of public service. Perhaps they were enunciated merely to convey the illusion of concerned attention. To the extent that this is true, the liberal profession will have failed; professional responsibility will have failed; and some other mechanism will be needed to meet the conditions of information and exercise.

Students of contract law may have detected here the equitable doctrine of promissory estoppel. Ordinarily, a gratuitous promise does not create a legal obligation. Not owing the money in any sense, W says to B that he will give B twenty dollars tomorrow. Other conditions being equal, no legal obligation is created. But if B has made it clear to W that he will be acting to his detriment in reliance upon W's promise, that he will be giving up something of value if W doesn't come through, then a legally binding obligation may be created. Suppose B were to say to W: "Because you will be giving me twenty dollars tomorrow, today I will put down a nonrefundable twenty-dollar deposit on a coat I have wanted, and I will promise the merchant to pay the balance tomorrow when I receive the money from you." At that point the law may well acknowledge a contract. When the maker of a promise ought reasonably to expect that the promise will induce a particular kind of action or forbearance on the part of the promisee, and where the promise does induce the action or forbearance, the obligation is no longer merely "moral": the promise may be held to be legally binding.[9]

In granting the legal profession monopoly status, the community relies to its detriment on the profession's collective representation that it will meet the conditions of information and exercise. The community loses something universally acknowledged to be of inestimable value if the legal profession fails to meet the responsibilities it has assumed in the process of professionalization. Of course, if we assume that the granting of monopoly status to the bar is the "consideration" that the bar receives in return for having agreed to meet the conditions of information and exercise, then the contract is a much more ordinary one. In either event, unlike the free-market pettifogger, professional attorneys have a clear duty to address the legal needs of nonparticipants; indeed, a duty to see to it that there are no nonparticipants. It is not a matter of gratuitous charity *pro bono publico*. It is a "basic tenet" of the bar's professional responsibility.

The Public Agency

The community takes the third approach to providing the intermediary between the lay public and the sophisticated adversarial system when it decides to employ attorneys directly, much as it does with fire fighters, judges, and police officers. If the interest that citizens have is important enough (it is difficult to think of a more important interest than civil justice), and if neither the free market nor the liberal profession can be relied on to do the job, the principal remaining option is directly to employ attorneys in organizations set up to provide legal services to the general public. Though lawyers will work for their clients (just as teachers work for their students), they will be paid by and will have some of their working conditions set by their employers—in this case, civil government. Where gratuitous charity and professional responsibility have failed, perhaps "conditions of employment" that are set by the community will succeed.

The most serious problem that can emerge within the public agency approach is, as the Preamble to the Model Rules notes, the compromising of professional autonomy, the damaging erosion of the bar's independence. Even though agency attorneys are nominally employed to provide legal services to the public, government officials may try to discourage these lawyers from bringing certain types of complaint—especially complaints against the government and its officials—even when the cases are legitimate. Government, the employer of attorneys, may be able to limit the degree to which citizens can challenge the state for having exceeded its

---

[9] *Fried v. Fisher*, 328 PA 497, 196 A 39 (1938).

proper authority. As the legal profession's "boss," it will do this by setting conditions of employment, both formal and informal, that restrict the types of case that can be brought to court. In controlling the legal profession—and thus access to the judiciary—the state can circumvent all legal limits to its authority. Though in some sense citizens may still "enjoy" legal rights against the community, they will not be able to appeal to the courts to obtain that which the law guarantees to them. Their rights will not have been secured.

Autonomy problems within legal-services agencies can be addressed by carefully attending to the structure of the organization. In universities, for example, the problem of unwarranted encroachment upon professional autonomy has been extensively dealt with under the general heading of "academic freedom." In practice, this entails a separation of administrative and professional functions within the institution so as to guarantee that academicians have the latitude that is required if they are to do their work. It is a secured limitation on the employer's right to determine the conditions and content of the professional's job. Substantial control is in the hands of members of the affected profession. By far the most important factor in securing professional autonomy within an employing organization is the type of association created by the professionals themselves.

We have seen how trade associations and professional associations are the characteristic organizations with respect to the two approaches discussed earlier. The social organization that can be expected to emerge among publicly employed attorneys is the public-sector labor union. Labor unions exist primarily to negotiate with the employer (in this case, the community) the terms and conditions of employment. The distinction drawn earlier between trade associations and professional associations parallels the two distinct sets of interests that can be furthered by a public-sector legal-services labor union. Employed attorneys may identify themselves as employees. They may feel that the work they are doing is not really their work but rather the agency's work; if the quality of service provided is low, that is not the employee's responsibility. Think of an assembly-line worker, building a poorly engineered product. "I am just doing a job, earning a living." To the extent that attorneys think of themselves in this way, the collective bargaining process will focus on "bread and butter" issues: wages, hours, and general working conditions. The employee's posture will be in essence "more money for less work," mirroring the employer's posture of "more work for less money."

On the other hand, attorneys may identify themselves as professionals; not being paid for their work but, in Haworth's words noted earlier, *in order that they may do their work.*[10] Employed professionals may focus not on their interests as employees, but on their interests as professionals with final responsibility for the quality of their work. Decent salaries and appropriate working conditions may be important, not because it is nice to earn more in better circumstances, but because adequate attention must be given to these matters if the agency and its professional staff are

---

[10] Lawrence Haworth, *Decadence and Objectivity* (Toronto: University of Toronto Press, 1978), p. 112.

to serve their public purpose. Likewise, if professional autonomy is under attack by administrators (or even by fellow professionals), the membership of a public-sector labor union has the option of placing those values high on its agenda in negotiations. Of course, where the community as a whole adequately appreciates the argument for an independent bar, it is unlikely that employer and employee will be at odds on this issue. Still, provided that lawyers in their roles as employees have not lost their sense of responsibility, labor unions can serve to further professionalism and buttress autonomy should the need arise to protect these critical values.

Suggestions for Further Reading

Law school courses in professional responsibility generally use weighty casebooks much like those employed in other law courses. A few of these are: Pirsig's *Professional Responsibility: Cases and Materials* (West Publishing Company); Morgan and Rotunda's *Professional Responsibility: Problems and Materials* (Foundation Press); Kaufman's *Problems in Professional Responsibility* (Little, Brown & Company); Mellinkoff's *Lawyers and the System of Justice* (West Publishing Company); Patterson and Cheatham's *The Profession of Law* (Foundation Press); and Countryman, Finman, and Schneyer's *The Lawyer in Modern Society* (Little, Brown & Company).

Other useful law school texts in somewhat different categories are: *The Lawyering Process* by Bellow and Moulton (Foundation Press), which gives some attention to ethical issues arising in clinical practice; and two paperback books: *Lawyers, Clients and Ethics* by Murray Teigh Bloom (Council on Legal Education for Professional Responsibility) and *Professional Responsibility: A Problem Approach* by Norman Redlich (Little, Brown & Company). The latter two contain useful problems and discussions.

A brief review of the teaching of ethics in law school is to be found in Michael J. Kelly's *Legal Ethics and Legal Education* (Institute of Society, Ethics and the Life Sciences).

Among the most useful monographs on legal ethics are David Mellinkoff's *The Conscience of a Lawyer* (West Publishing Company), Monroe Freedman's *Lawyers' Ethics in an Adversary System* (The Bobbs-Merrill Company, Inc.), and Geoffrey Hazard's *Ethics in the Practice of Law* (Yale University Press). Also worth mentioning is Henry S. Drinker's *Legal Ethics* (Columbia University Press).

Three helpful anthologies of writings on legal ethics are: *Professional Responsibility: A Guide for Attorneys* (American Bar Association); *Lawyer's Ethics,* edited by Allan Gerson (Transaction Books); and *The Good Lawyer,* edited by David Luban (Rowman & Allanheld). Luban's book contains a good deal of philosophical material.

Beyond the articles cited in earlier chapters, the reader may wish to review the following:

Charles P. Curtis, "The Ethics of Advocacy," *Stanford Law Review* 4 (1951): 3–23.

Michael Davis, "Conflict of Interest," *Business and Professional Ethics Journal* 1:4 (Summer 1982): 17–27.

Henry S. Drinker, "Some Remarks on Mr. Curtis' 'The Ethics of Advocacy,'" *Stanford Law Review* 4 (1952): 349–357.

Marvin Frankel, "The Search for Truth: An Umpireal View," *University of Pennsylvania Law Review* 123 (1975): 1031–1059.

Charles Fried, "The Lawyer as Friend: The Moral Foundations of the Lawyer-Client Relation," *Yale Law Journal* 85 (1976): 1060–1089.

Virginia Held, "The Division of Moral Labor and the Role of the Lawyer," in David Luban, ed., *The Good Lawyer* (Totowa: Rowman & Allenheld, 1984), pp. 60–79.

David Luban, "The Adversary System Excuse," in David Luban, ed., *The Good Lawyer* (Totowa: Rowman & Allanheld, 1984), pp. 83–122.

Lester J. Mazor, "Power and Responsibility in the Attorney-Client Relation," *Stanford Law Review* 20 (1968): 1120–1139.

Gerald J. Postema, "Moral Responsibility in Professional Ethics," in Wade Robison, Michael S. Pritchard, and Joseph Elllin, eds., *Profits and Professions* (Clifton: Humana Press, 1983), pp. 37–63.

William H. Simon, "The Ideology of Advocacy: Procedural Justice and Professional Ethics," *Wisconsin Law Review* (1978): 29–144.

Among the many nontechnical books criticizing the legal profession are:

Fred Rodell, *Woe Unto You, Lawyers,* 2nd ed. (New York: Pageant Press, 1957).

Robert Lefcourt, *Law Against the People* (New York: Random House, Inc., 1971).

Ralph Nader and Mark Green, *Verdicts on Lawyers* (New York: Thomas Y. Crowell, 1976).

Jethro K. Lieberman, *Crisis at the Bar: Lawyers' Unethical Conduct and What to Do About It* (New York: W. W. Norton & Co., Inc., 1978).

Philip Stern, *Lawyers on Trial* (New York: New York Times Books, 1980).

David Kairys, *The Politics of Law* (New York: Pantheon Books, 1982).

Additional references are described in *Legal Ethics: An Annotated Bibliography and Resource Guide* by Frederick A. Elliston and Jane Van Schaick (Littleton, Colorado: Fred B. Rothman & Co., 1984).

Index